P9-CMU-350

APPARITIONS

Property of
Scarborough School Dept.
Title I
Room 151 Book No. 1

SCARBOROUGH SCHOOL DEPT
TITLE I

SCARBOROUGH PUBLIC LIBRARY
TILLEY

CRITICAL READING SERIES

APPARITIONS

21 Stories of Ghosts, Spirits, and Mysterious Manifestations—with Exercises for Developing Reading Comprehension and Critical Thinking Skills

Henry Billings

Melissa Billings

John F. Warner

Margaret B. Warner

JAMESTOWN  PUBLISHERS

a division of NTC/CONTEMPORARY PUBLISHING GROUP

Lincolnwood, Illinois USA

ISBN 0-89061-110-6

Published by Jamestown Publishers,
a division of NTC/Contemporary Publishing Group, Inc.
4255 West Touhy Avenue
Lincolnwood (Chicago), Illinois 60646-1975, U.S.A.
© 1999 NTC/Contemporary Publishing Group, Inc.
All rights reserved.
No part of this publication may be reproduced, stored in a retrieval
system, or transmitted in any form or by any means without the prior
written permission of the publisher.

90 VL 098765432

CONTENTS

UNIT THREE

To the Student

Our lives are mysteries. Why are we here? What happens to us after we die? It is natural for us to wonder about the answers to these basic questions. Perhaps that is the reason why stories about spirits who communicate to the living from beyond the grave are so fascinating. We think they may shed some light on what is in store for us.

The articles in this book present accounts of moments when the living have supposedly caught glimpses of the life after this one. However, they are not ghost stories in the usual sense. They are not meant to frighten you. Instead, they should encourage you to think. Unlike scary ghost stories you might hear repeated around a campfire late at night, these articles are like stories you read in a newspaper. They strive to present the facts as they have been reported. They allow you, the reader, to consider opposing points of view and make your own decisions about who is telling the truth and who is mistaken—or lying.

As you read and enjoy the 21 articles in this book, you will also be developing your reading skills. *Apparitions* is for students who already read fairly well but who want to read faster and to increase their understanding of what they read. If you complete the 21 lessons—reading the articles and completing the exercises—you will surely increase your reading speed and improve your reading comprehension and critical thinking skills. Also, because these exercises include items of the types often found on state and national tests, learning how to complete them will prepare you for tests you may have to take in the future.

How to Use This Book

About the Book. *Apparitions* contains three units, each of which includes seven lessons. Each lesson begins with an article about an unusual event, person, or group. The article is followed by a group of four reading comprehension exercises and a set of three critical thinking exercises. The reading comprehension exercises will help you understand the article. The critical thinking exercises will help you think about what you have read and how it relates to your own experience.

At the end of each lesson, you will also have the opportunity to give your personal response to some aspect of the article and then to assess how well you understood what you read.

The Sample Lesson.   Working through the sample lesson, the first lesson in the book, with your class or group will demonstrate how a lesson is organized. The sample lesson explains how to complete the exercises and score your answers. The correct answers for the sample exercises and sample scores are printed in lighter type. In some cases, explanations of the correct answers are given. The explanations will help you understand how to think through these question types.

If you have any questions about how to complete the exercises or score them, this is the time to get the answers.

Working Through Each Lesson.   Begin each lesson by looking at the photographs and reading the captions. Before you read, predict what you think the article will be about. Then read the article.

Sometimes your teacher may decide to time your reading. Timing helps you keep track of and increase your reading speed. If you have been timed, enter your reading time in the box at the end of the lesson. Then use the Words-per-Minute Table to find your reading speed, and record your speed on the Reading Speed graph at the end of the unit.

Next complete the Reading Comprehension and Critical Thinking exercises. The directions for each exercise will tell you how to mark your answers. When you have finished all four Reading Comprehension exercises, use the answer key provided by your teacher to check your work. Follow the directions after each exercise to find your score. Record your Reading Comprehension scores on the graph at the end of each unit. Then check your answers to the Author's Approach, Summarizing and Paraphrasing, and Critical Thinking exercises. Fill in the Critical Thinking chart at the end of each unit with your evaluation of your work and comments about your progress.

At the end of each unit you will also complete a Compare/Contrast chart. The completed chart will help you see what the articles have in common, and it will give you an opportunity to explore your own attitudes toward the subject of supernatural occurrences, life after death, and apparitions.

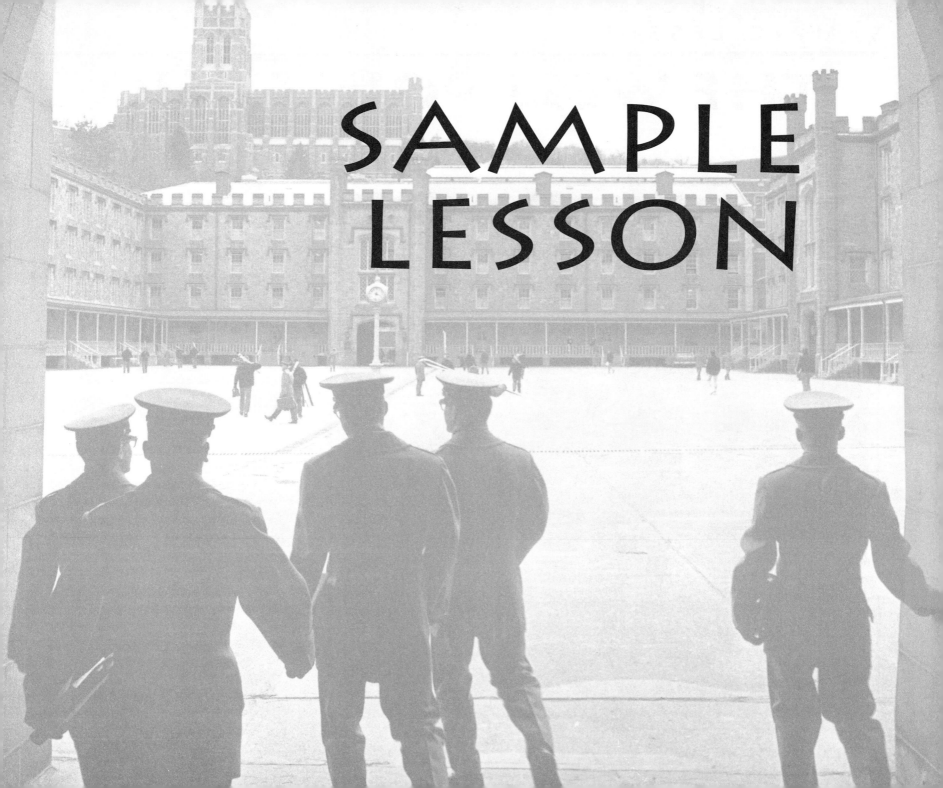

SAMPLE
LESSON

THE WEST POINT GHOST

This view of the U.S. Military Academy at West Point shows the South Barracks and Chapel. The West Point Ghost supposedly haunted room 4714 in the 47th Division Barracks.

Cadet Captain Keith W. Bakken did not believe in ghosts. But what other explanation could there be? This was one mystery that had him baffled.

2 On the night of October 21, 1972, Captain Bakken was asleep in his room at West Point, the U.S. Military Academy on the Hudson River in New York, when a series of loud shouts rudely awakened him. He leaped out of bed and dashed down the hall to Room 4714, the source of the shouts. There Captain Bakken found two terrified cadets. "What's going on here?" Captain Bakken demanded. "We've…we've seen a…a ghost!" the cadets stammered. Then they told their astonishing story.

3 Both cadets had been sound asleep when they were awakened by a strange noise. At the same time, they felt a chill in the room. Then a ghostly figure floated through the door. Both cadets swore that the figure was a soldier dressed in an old-time uniform. He wore a handlebar mustache and carried a musket.

4 Cadet Captain Bakken did not know what to make of the eerie tale. Were the

men lying? He doubted it. West Point was the oldest military school in the United States, with a fine reputation to uphold. Only the cream of the crop were admitted. Since its founding in 1802, it had produced many of the nation's leaders. In fact, two presidents were West Point graduates. What's more, all West Point cadets lived by the Honor System. Lying, cheating, or stealing would mean immediate dismissal. No, the two cadets would not risk their careers for the sake of a childish prank. Besides, Captain Bakken thought, they seemed genuinely frightened. And the room *did* feel quite cold.

5   Wanting to see for himself what was going on, Captain Bakken decided to spend the rest of the night in the room. But the ghost—or whatever it was—did not return.

6   The next night he asked another cadet to share the room with him. About 2:00 A.M. the ghost returned. Both men saw "a figure partially extended out of the wall," as they later described it. Although it vanished in a short time, the men were sure the ghostly figure wore an old-time uniform. What is more, they agreed that the room had felt "icy-cold."

7   Word of the ghost soon spread throughout the Point. Soon cadets who had been assigned to Room 4714 in past years came forward. They, too, they said, had felt a presence—a ghost—in the room. A trip to the library yielded more information. Uniforms like the one worn by the ghost were standard for soldiers in the 1830s!

8   The story eventually found its way to the newspapers. "Ghost Haunts West Point!" screamed the headlines. West Point leaders were upset by the stories. It was not the kind of publicity they wanted for the school. The Point's commanding general declared Room 4714 off limits to everyone. All the furniture was removed and the door was padlocked.

9   As the Christmas holidays drew near, interest in the ghost died down. No more stories appeared in newspapers. Even many of the cadets seemed to forget about it. Then a midshipman from the Point's rival, the U.S. Naval Academy, at Annapolis, Maryland, stepped forward.

10   The ghost was a Halloween prank, stated Midshipman William Gravell. He confessed to being the one behind the hoax. The "ghost," he said, was nothing more than a picture he had projected on a wall of Room 4714. What about the ice-cold room? That was nothing more than carbon dioxide shot from a fire extinguisher, Midshipman Gravell explained. Then he smiled, for he was pleased with himself. The prank, he admitted, had been more successful than he had hoped.

11   And that ends the story of the West Point ghost. Or does it? Of course, the cadets at the Point hated to think they had been fooled by someone from their

These West Point Cadets and Cadet Officers are wearing uniforms from 1842, about the same time period as the uniform worn by the West Point Ghost.

rival academy. The ghost had to be real, they said. Too many cadets claimed to have seen the apparition. Besides, there were just too many holes in the midshipman's story. For one thing, the Point in New York and the Naval Academy in Maryland are about four hundred miles apart. How could Gravell have traveled that distance on so many occasions without being missed at school? What's more, how could he have hidden himself and the projector inside Room 4714? Surely someone would have seen him. No, the cadets argued, Midshipman Gravell could not have done what he claimed.

12   *The Pointer*, a student newspaper, offered these possible explanations. About a hundred years ago, a West Point officer died in a house fire. The house stood not far from the site of the 47th Division Barracks—the building in which Room 4714 is situated. Perhaps the ghost was that of the dead soldier? Or perhaps it was the ghost of a restless soul from an old burial ground nearby?

13   The apparition has not reappeared since 1972. Room 4714 was reopened in 1978, and there have been no further reports of the ghostly soldier. So perhaps it was the product of a hoax after all. On the other hand, who was responsible and how did they pull it off? Unless it appears again, we may never know the truth behind the West Point ghost.

If you have been timed while reading this article, enter your reading time below. Then turn to the Words-per-Minute Table on page 71 and look up your reading speed (words per minute). Enter your reading speed on the graph on page 72.

Reading Time: Sample Lesson

_____ : _____
Minutes   Seconds

Finding the Main Idea

One statement below expresses the main idea of the article. One statement is too general, or too broad. The other statement explains only part of the article; it is too narrow. Label the statements using the following key:

M—Main Idea   **B—Too Broad**   **N—Too Narrow**

_____B_____ 1. Strange, unexplained occurrences have taken place at the U.S. Military Academy. [This statement is true, but it is *too broad*. The story is about particular strange occurrences—the sightings of a ghost.]

_____N_____ 2. The West Point ghost appeared to be the ghost of a soldier from the last century. [This statement is true, but it is *too narrow*. It gives only one piece of information from the story.]

_____M_____ 3. The reported appearance of a ghostly soldier at West Point in 1972 caused an uproar, and no one has ever been able to determine what caused the apparition. [This statement is the *main idea*. It tells you what the reading selection is about—a ghost at West Point. It also tells you that the mystery of the ghost was never solved.]

___15___	Score 15 points for a correct M answer.
___10___	Score 5 points for each correct B or N answer.
___25___	**Total Score:** Finding the Main Idea

 Recalling Facts

How well do you remember the facts in the article? Put an X in the box next to the answer that correctly completes each statement about the article.

1. William Gravell was a
   ☐ a. captain at West Point.
   ☒ b. student at the U.S. Naval Academy.
   ☐ c. newspaper reporter.

2. The Honor System requires cadets to
   ☒ a. be honest.
   ☐ b. respect their superiors.
   ☐ c. be brave.

3. Room 4714 was
   ☒ a. in the 47th Division Barracks.
   ☐ b. on the site of a burial ground.
   ☐ c. Captain Bakken's room.

4. Everyone who saw it said that the ghost
   ☒ a. carried a musket.
   ☐ b. was dressed as a Revolutionary War soldier.
   ☐ c. wore a gray uniform.

5. The U.S. Military Academy is located in
   ☐ a. California.
   ☐ b. Maryland.
   ☒ c. New York.

Score 5 points for each correct answer.

___25___ **Total Score:** Recalling Facts

C | Making Inferences

When you combine your own experience and information from a text to draw a conclusion that is not directly stated in that text, you are making an inference. Below are five statements that may or may not be inferences based on information in the article. Label the statements using the following key:

C—Correct Inference   **F—Faulty Inference**

_____C_____ 1. West Point officials guarded the reputation of the school carefully. [This is a *correct* inference. You are told in the story that the officials at the school were upset by newspaper reports of the ghost, because the stories did not provide the kind of publicity they wanted for the school.]

_____F_____ 2. Keith Bakken believed that the West Point ghost was a real ghost, not part of a hoax. [This is a *faulty* inference. There is nothing in the story to indicate whether Captain Bakken believed that the ghost was real or not.]

_____C_____ 3. One of the goals of a West Point education is to produce leaders who are honest. [This is a *correct* inference. The article states that all cadets are required to live by a code of honor that forbids lying, cheating, and stealing.]

_____F_____ 4. People have given up trying to find out whether the West Point ghost was real or not. [This is a *faulty* inference. The questions remain unanswered. The fact that stories are being written about it today suggests that many people are still curious about the apparition.]

> Score 5 points for each correct answer.
>
> ____20____ **Total Score:** Making Inferences

D | Using Words Precisely

Each numbered sentence below contains an underlined word or phrase from the article. Following the sentence are three definitions. One definition is closest to the meaning of the underlined word. One definition is opposite or nearly opposite. Label those two definitions using the following key. Do not label the remaining definition.

C—Closest   **O—Opposite or Nearly Opposite**

1. "We've...we've seen a...a ghost!" the cadets <u>stammered</u>.

    _____ a. yelled loudly

    ___C___ b. said falteringly

    ___O___ c. stated clearly

2. Cadet Captain Bakken did not know what to make of the <u>eerie</u> tale.

    _____ a. ridiculous

    ___C___ b. weird

    ___O___ c. sensible

3. Besides, Captain Bakken thought, they seemed <u>genuinely</u> frightened.

    ___C___ a. truly

    _____ b. sadly

    ___O___ c. falsely

4. A trip to the library <u>yielded</u> more information.

    ___C___ a. produced

    ___O___ b. used up

    _____ c. misrepresented

5. Then a midshipman from the Point's <u>rival</u>, the U.S. Naval Academy, at Annapolis, Maryland, stepped forward.

_____O_____   a. partner

_____   b. department

_____C_____   c. competitor

---

    15   Score 3 points for each correct C answer.

    10   Score 2 points for each correct O answer.

    25   **Total Score:** Using Words Precisely

Enter the four total scores in the spaces below, and add them together to find your Reading Comprehension Score. Then record your score on the graph on page 73.

Score	Question Type	Sample Lesson
25	Finding the Main Idea	
25	Recalling Facts	
25	Making Inferences	
25	Using Words Precisely	
100	**Reading Comprehension Score**	

Author's Approach

Put an X in the box next to the correct answer.

1. The main purpose of the first paragraph is to
   - ☐ a. inform the reader about Captain Bakken.
   - ☒ b. encourage the reader to keep reading to find out about the mystery.
   - ☐ c. persuade the reader that ghosts were responsible for the mystery.

2. From the statements below, choose those that you believe the author would agree with.
   - ☐ a. The West Point cadets who claimed they saw the ghost were in on Midshipman Gravell's prank.
   - ☒ b. The truth about the West Point ghost will probably never be known.
   - ☒ c. Students at West Point are proud of their reputation and their traditions.

3. Choose the statement below that is the weakest argument for claiming that the West Point ghost was not a hoax.
   - ☐ a. Someone would have seen Midshipman Gravell and his projector in Room 4714.
   - ☐ b. Gravell could not have traveled such a long distance on so many occasions without being missed at his school.
   - ☒ c. The apparition has not reappeared since Gravell confessed to being the one behind the ghost.

---

    3   Number of correct answers

Record your personal assessment of your work on the Critical Thinking Chart on page 74.

Summarizing and Paraphrasing

Put an X in the box next to the correct answer.

1. Below are summaries of the article. Choose the summary that says all the most important things about the article but in the fewest words.

☐ a. A ghost dressed in a soldier's uniform from the 1830s appeared to some West Point cadets. [This summary leaves out several important details from the article.]

☐ b. Several West Point cadets claimed that they had seen a ghost in Room 4714. Soon after the ghost stories became public, a midshipman from the U.S. Naval Academy confessed to masterminding the ghost hoax. West Point cadets refused to believe him and have offered their own explanations. [This summary says all the most important things about the article but includes too many unnecessary details.]

☒ c. After a ghost supposedly appeared to several West Point cadets, a student from a rival school claimed responsibility for the prank. The cadets don't believe the ghost was a hoax and have suggested other explanations. [This summary says all the most important things about the article in the fewest words.]

2. Read the statement about the article below. Then read the paraphrase of that statement. Choose the reason that best tells why the paraphrase does not say the same thing as the statement.

Statement: The leaders of West Point wanted to put an end to the publicity about the ghost sightings because such stories, they believed, tarnished the school's serious reputation.

Paraphrase: West Point leaders didn't want the school's reputation hurt.

☐ a. Paraphrase says too much.

☒ b. Paraphrase doesn't say enough. [The paraphrase summarizes part of the statement but neglects to mention the unwanted publicity about the ghost sightings.]

☐ c. Paraphrase doesn't agree with the statement about the article.

_____2_____ Number of correct answers

Record your personal assessment of your work on the Critical Thinking Chart on page 74.

Critical Thinking

Put an X in the box next to the correct answer for questions 1, 3, 4, and 5. Follow the directions provided for the other question.

1. From the article, you can predict that if Midshipman Gravell really had been responsible for the "ghost," his fellow students would have

☒ a. congratulated him on his successful prank.

☐ b. been disappointed in him.

☐ c. apologized to the students at West Point.

2. Choose from the letters below to correctly complete the following statement. Write the letters on the lines.

In the article, ___a___ and ___c___ are alike.

a. the ghost described by the occupants of Room 4714

b. William Gravell's description of the ghost

c. Cadet Captain Bakken's description of the ghost

3. What was the cause of the decision to declare Room 4714 off limits?

☒ a. Too many stories about the West Point ghost began to appear in newspapers.

☐ b. All the furniture in the room was removed.

☐ c. Interest in the ghost died down.

CRITICAL THINKING

4. If you were a cadet captain at West Point, how could you best use the information in the article to react to a cadet's sighting of a ghost?

- ☐ a. Try to get as much publicity as possible for your school by leaking the story to the newspapers.

- ☒ b. Follow Bakken's example: take the story seriously and try to find out for yourself what was going on.

- ☐ c. Realize that the story must be silenced quickly and dismiss the student for violating the Honor System.

5. What did you have to do to answer question 2?

- ☐ a. find a cause (why something happened)

- ☒ b. find a comparison (how things are the same)

- ☐ c. draw a conclusion (a sensible statement based on the text and your experience)

_____5_____ Number of correct answers

Record your personal assessment of your work on the Critical Thinking Chart on page 74.

Personal Response

What was most surprising or interesting to you about this article?

[Explain what you found intriguing or unexpected in the article.]

_____

_____

_____

Self-Assessment

From reading this article, I have learned

[Record any idea or fact that you learned from the article.]

_____

_____

_____

CRITICAL THINKING

Self-Assessment

To get the most out of the Critical Reading series program, you need to take charge of your own progress in improving your reading comprehension and critical thinking skills. Here are some of the features that help you work on those essential skills.

Reading Comprehension Exercises. Complete these exercises immediately after reading the article. They help you recall what you have read, understand the stated and implied main ideas, and add words to your working vocabulary.

Critical Thinking Skills Exercises. These exercises help you focus on the author's approach and purpose, recognize and generate summaries and paraphrases, and identify relationships between ideas.

Personal Response and Self-assessment. Questions in this category help you relate the articles to your personal experience and give you the opportunity to evaluate your understanding of the information in that lesson.

Compare and Contrast Charts. At the end of each unit you will complete a Compare and Contrast chart. The completed chart helps you see what the articles have in common and gives you an opportunity to explore your own ideas about the topics discussed in the articles.

The Graphs. The graphs and charts at the end of each unit enable you to keep track of your progress. Check your graphs regularly with your teacher. Decide whether your progress is satisfactory or whether you need additional work on some skills. What types of exercises are you having difficulty with? Talk with your teacher about ways to work on the skills in which you need the most practice.

UNIT ONE

THE BELL WITCH

This countryside in Robertson County, Tennessee, is the location of the Bell farm and cabin.

"O uch!" Twelve-year-old Betsy Bell put her hand to her face. "Stop it!" she screamed, jumping in pain. Both Betsy's cheeks were flaming, as if someone had slapped her across the face. But who—or what—could have done the slapping? That was the mystery. For Betsy was all alone in the room.

2 It was not the first time Betsy had been hurt by an invisible attacker. For several weeks, she and other members of the Bell family had been tormented. Their beds were torn apart. Their hair was pulled, their noses were pinched, and their faces were slapped.

3 According to Williams Bell, Betsy's brother, the trouble started in 1817, on a warm Indian summer's night in Tennessee. John Bell and his wife, Lucy, and their eight children had finished supper. Then, as was their custom, they gathered around the hearth. John Bell, a staunch Baptist, liked to read to the family from the Bible. But on this night, loud rapping and scraping noises interrupted his reading. John Bell stared at his children. "Quiet!" he said sternly. "This is no time for pranks."

4 The children looked up at him innocently. "We did nothing, Father," said

Joel. John Bell tried to continue his reading, but the noises persisted. Now he truly looked angry. "Really, Father," said John, Jr., "the noises are coming from outside." The boy was right. It was as if someone were clawing at the doors and windows of the house, trying to get in.

5   After that, the noises were heard every night. Soon they moved indoors. There were sounds of rats gnawing on wood and of a dog's claws scraping across the floor. Wood seemed to crack and splinter, as if the beds were being torn apart. Then the noises became human. Strangling and choking sounds seemed to come from everywhere. But although the Bells searched the house from top to bottom, they could find nothing amiss.

6   The Bells kept their problem a secret for almost a year. John Bell was a respected farmer, and he was afraid people would think he was crazy if he told what was going on. But when his children were attacked, he decided to get help. He invited James Johnson, a neighbor who was a lay preacher, to the farm.

7   Astonished at the sounds he heard, Johnson was convinced that an evil spirit was at work. "Stop, I beseech you, in the name of the Lord!" he commanded. To everyone's surprise, the noises did stop. But they soon started again, even louder than before. In fact, they were so loud that they fairly shook the house. What is more, the attacks on the Bells became even more vicious.

8   By that time, news of the strange happenings at the Bell farm had spread throughout Robertson County. Every night the house filled with people who wanted to hear the noises for themselves. They were not disappointed. The source of the noises remained invisible, but along with the sounds, soft whispers began to be heard. At first the words were difficult to understand. Then, gradually, whole sentences became clear.

9   Of course, now that the presence could speak, listeners asked it to explain who and what it was. A number of answers were given.

10   "I am a spirit from everywhere—heaven, hell, the earth," the voice said. "I am in the air, in houses—any place at any time. I have been created for millions of years." Another time it said, "I am a spirit. I was once very happy, but I have been disturbed."

11   The spirit told its audience a number of wild tales. But the story that most interested people concerned a local woman who was thought by many people to be a witch. "I am the spirit of old Kate Batts," said the voice one evening.

12   Kate Batts had once done business with John Bell. Claiming afterward that Bell had cheated her, Kate vowed revenge. "I'll get him!" she swore to all who would listen. But the townspeople were used to Kate's evil tongue. She was stubborn and bad-tempered. As a result, she had many enemies. People loved the idea that the spirit claimed to be that of old Kate. It did not matter that the woman was still alive. From then on, the spirit was referred to as Kate, The Bell Witch.

13   Not everyone believed in the spirit, though. Since most of the violence was directed at Betsy, it was suggested that she might be causing the problem. Betsy was accused of ventriloquism, or "throwing her voice." John, Jr., suggested a test to see if this was true. He asked a visiting doctor to place his hand over Betsy's mouth at a time when the voice was speaking. The doctor did, and he declared that Betsy certainly was not making the sounds.

14   There was other proof of Betsy's innocence. Hoping to spare her further torture from the spirit, the Bells sent Betsy to live with neighbors. But there, too, she was tormented. And while she was away, the Bell household continued to be attacked. There was no way Betsy could have caused the occurrences at the farm. But a spirit could easily manage to trouble two places, said believers.

15   At some point the Bell Witch tired of Betsy and turned its attentions to John

A marker along a Tennessee roadside relates the legend of the Bell Witch.

Bell. Bell's tongue grew stiff and swollen, so he could neither eat nor speak for hours. The spirit seemed to enjoy John Bell's suffering. "I will torment you into your grave!" she threatened.

16 Kate's nature was not all evil, however. She loved to quote from the Bible. When ministers visited the Bell farm, she would talk with them at length. She prayed and even sang hymns. Those who heard her said she had a charming voice.

17 At times Kate even made herself useful. One night Lucy Bell wondered aloud whether her son Jesse had yet returned from a trip. "Wait a minute, Lucy, I'll go and see for you," said Kate. A few seconds later, she returned with a report. "He's home," she said. "He's sitting at a table reading by the light of a candle." Jesse, who lived a mile away, later confirmed Kate's report.

18 Lucy Bell was a favorite of Kate's. When Lucy became ill, the spirit brought her gifts. She cracked nuts and dropped them onto the bed. She brought oranges, bananas, and grapes—fruits that in those days could not be found in Tennessee. Kate claimed she had gotten them in the West Indies.

19 About that time, Betsy Bell fell in love with a young man named Joshua Gardner. The Bells were delighted with the match. Kate, however, was not. "Betsy Bell," she said, "do not marry Joshua Gardner." At first the spirit pleaded sweetly. But when Betsy ignored the warnings, Kate grew furious. She did everything she could to break up their romance.

20 Kate also began a serious attack on John Bell, whom she called "Old Jack." The poor man became very ill. The doctors could find no cure. Finally, on December 19, 1820, Williams found his father in a coma. By his side was a vial of strange-looking liquid. When it was tested on the family cat, the animal died almost at once. Their worst fears were realized: poison.

21 "I put it there!" cried Kate. "I gave Old Jack a big dose of it last night while he was asleep, which fixed him." John Bell died the next morning, as Kate shouted and sang with glee. She had made good on her threat to torment John Bell to his grave.

22 For a while after John Bell's death, the spirit visited less often. The Bells began to think that life might return to normal. However, when Betsy and Joshua became engaged, Kate again plagued the couple. She said so many horrid things to them in front of their friends that they were embarrassed to be seen in public. Finally Betsy had had enough. She broke her engagement.

23 This seemed to satisfy Kate, for that spring she announced that she was leaving. Before she left, however, she made one more threat. "Good-bye," she called out, "I leave for now. But I will return in several years." With that, something like a cannon ball rolled down the chimney and burst into smoke. Kate had plagued the Bell family for four long years. At last, they were once again at peace.

24 Seven years later, however, the spirit kept her promise. She returned to the Bell farm and for two weeks scratched at the doors and windows. Needless to say, the Bells were terrified. Luckily, this time Kate didn't enter the house. However, she did visit the home of John Bell, Jr., who had married and started a family of his own. She had a message to deliver. "I will be back in 107 years!" she declared. Then she left.

25 Well, 107 years have come and gone. So far Kate has not made another grand appearance at the Bell farm. But the people of Robertson County swear that she never left. Strange, unexplainable occurrences continue to this day. Many of them center around a cave at the edge of the Bell farm. People have reported seeing the figure of a woman floating through the cave. The Bell Witch is pretty much an accepted resident of the area. Whenever something unusual happens, folks just shrug and say, "Kate probably did it."

If you have been timed while reading this article, enter your reading time below. Then turn to the Words-per-Minute Table on page 71 and look up your reading speed (words per minute). Enter your reading speed on the graph on page 72.

Reading Time: Lesson 1

_____ : _____
Minutes   Seconds

A | Finding the Main Idea

One statement below expresses the main idea of the article. One statement is too general, or too broad. The other statement explains only part of the article; it is too narrow. Label the statements using the following key:

M—Main Idea   **B—Too Broad**   **N—Too Narrow**

_____ 1. Kate tormented John Bell to his grave.

_____ 2. The Bell family was tormented for years by a wicked spirit known as Kate.

_____ 3. The Bell family were victims of seemingly supernatural occurrences.

_____ Score 15 points for a correct M answer.

_____ Score 5 points for each correct B or N answer.

_____ **Total Score:** Finding the Main Idea

B | Recalling Facts

How well do you remember the facts in the article? Put an X in the box next to the answer that correctly completes each statement about the article.

1. The story of The Bell Witch takes place in
   □ a. Georgia.
   □ b. South Carolina.
   □ c. Tennessee.

2. John Bell and his wife, Lucy, had
   □ a. two children.
   □ b. six children.
   □ c. eight children.

3. John Bell was a
   □ a. farmer.
   □ b. lay preacher.
   □ c. doctor.

4. Kate Batts was
   □ a. John Bell's sister.
   □ b. a woman John Bell had once done business with.
   □ c. James Johnson's wife.

5. When the spirit left the second time, it promised that it would return in
   □ a. 7 years.
   □ b. 100 years.
   □ c. 107 years.

_____ Score 5 points for each correct answer.

_____ **Total Score:** Recalling Facts

C | Making Inferences

When you combine your own experience and information from a text to draw a conclusion that is not directly stated in that text, you are making an inference. Below are five statements that may or may not be inferences based on information in the article. Label the statements using the following key:

C—Correct Inference   F—Faulty Inference

_____   1. Williams Bell thought the spirit was a hoax.

_____   2. Betsy Bell never married.

_____   3. Kate Batts lied when she said that John Bell had cheated her.

_____   4. The spirit made a strong impression on Williams Bell.

_____   5. Bell's neighbors were convinced that the spirit was dangerous to them.

Score 5 points for each correct answer.

_____ **Total Score:** Making Inferences

D | Using Words Precisely

Each numbered sentence below contains an underlined word or phrase from the article. Following the sentence are three definitions. One definition is closest to the meaning of the underlined word. One definition is opposite or nearly opposite. Label those two definitions using the following key. Do not label the remaining definition.

C—Closest   O—Opposite or Nearly Opposite

1. "The blows were distinctly heard," Betsy's brother Williams later wrote.

    _____   a. never

    _____   b. clearly

    _____   c. vaguely

2. John Bell, a staunch Baptist, liked to read to the family from the Bible.

    _____   a. strict

    _____   b. educated

    _____   c. careless

3. John Bell tried to continue his reading, but the noises persisted.

    _____   a. stopped

    _____   b. continued

    _____   c. grew louder

4. But although the Bells searched the house from top to bottom, they could find nothing amiss.

    _____   a. right

    _____   b. new

    _____   c. wrong

5. Jesse, who lived a mile away, later <u>confirmed</u> Kate's report.

_____ a. burned

_____ b. denied

_____ c. verified

_____ Score 3 points for each correct C answer.

_____ Score 2 points for each correct O answer.

_____ **Total Score:** Using Words Precisely

Enter the four total scores in the spaces below, and add them together to find your Reading Comprehension Score. Then record your score on the graph on page 73.

Score	Question Type	Lesson 1
_____	Finding the Main Idea	
_____	Recalling Facts	
_____	Making Inferences	
_____	Using Words Precisely	
_____	**Reading Comprehension Score**	

Author's Approach

Put an X in the box next to the correct answer.

1. The main purpose of the first paragraph is to
   - ☐ a. describe Betsy Bell.
   - ☐ b. persuade the reader that Betsy was faking the attack.
   - ☐ c. inform the reader about a mysterious force that attacked Betsy.

2. Which of the following statements from the article best describes the Bell Witch's attitude toward those she haunted?
   - ☐ a. "The spirit seemed to enjoy John Bell's suffering."
   - ☐ b. "She loved to quote from the Bible."
   - ☐ c. "Those who heard her said she had a charming voice."

3. What does the author imply by saying "When it [the liquid in the vial] was tested on the family cat, the animal died almost at once"?
   - ☐ a. The Bell family blamed the ghost for the death of their cat.
   - ☐ b. The Bell family was cruel to all their pets.
   - ☐ c. The poison in the liquid must have been very strong.

4. The author tells this story mainly by
   - ☐ a. retelling the Bell family's personal experiences with the Bell witch.
   - ☐ b. comparing the Bell witch with other spirits in Robertson County.
   - ☐ c. telling several families' experiences with the Bell witch.

_____ Number of correct answers

Record your personal assessment of your work on the Critical Thinking Chart on page 74.

Summarizing and Paraphrasing

Follow the directions provided for questions 1 and 2. Put an X in the box next to the correct answer for question 3.

1. Look for the important ideas and events in paragraphs 3 and 4. Summarize those paragraphs in one or two sentences.

_____

_____

_____

2. Complete the following one-sentence summary of the article using the lettered phrases from the phrase bank below. Write the letters on the lines.

Phrase Bank:
a. the first time the spirit visited the Bell family
b. Kate's promise to return
c. the mischief the spirit caused

After a short introduction, the article about the Bell Witch describes _____, goes on to explain _____, and ends with _____.

3. Read the statement about the article below. Then read the paraphrase of that statement. Choose the reason that best tells why the paraphrase does not say the same thing as the statement.

Statement: Although Kate announced that she was leaving Bell farm more than 100 years ago, some people in Robertson County claim that she never left.

Paraphrase: Kate left Bell farm more than 100 years ago, but she promised to return.

☐ a. Paraphrase says too much.

☐ b. Paraphrase doesn't say enough.

☐ c. Paraphrase doesn't agree with the statement about the article.

_____ Number of correct answers

Record your personal assessment of your work on the Critical Thinking Chart on page 74.

Critical Thinking

Put an X in the box next to the correct answer for questions 1 and 4. Follow the directions provided for questions 2 and 3.

1. From the article, you can predict that if Betsy had married Joshua Gardner,

☐ a. Kate would have killed Lucy Bell.

☐ b. Kate would not have stopped haunting the Bell family.

☐ c. Kate would still have left the Bell family for seven years.

CRITICAL THINKING

2. Choose from the letters below to correctly complete the following statement. Write the letters on the lines.

In the article, _____ and _____ are different.

   a. Kate's treatment of Betsy

   b. Kate's treatment of Lucy

   c. Kate's treatment of John

3. Read paragraph 20. Then choose from the letters below to correctly complete the following statement. Write the letters on the lines.

According to paragraph 20, _____ happened because _____.

   a. John's death

   b. Kate called him "Old Jack"

   c. he had taken poison

4. What did you have to do to answer question 2?

   ☐ a. find a cause (why something happened)

   ☐ b. find a comparison (how things are the same)

   ☐ c. find a contrast (how things are different)

_____ Number of correct answers

Record your personal assessment of your work on the Critical Thinking Chart on page 74.

Personal Response

A question I would like answered by Betsy Bell is

_____

_____

_____

_____

Self-Assessment

I can't really understand how

_____

_____

_____

_____

CRITICAL THINKING

THE GRAY MAN OF PAWLEY'S ISLAND

The Gray Man is no ordinary ghost. In fact, to the people who live on Pawley's Island, South Carolina, he is a hero. It is said that he has saved thousands of lives.

2   The Gray Man hardly looks like a champion, however. He is short and skinny. He dresses in odd-looking clothes—a gray suit with a long jacket, and a hat shaped like a turtle shell. He does have one remarkable feature, though—he is faceless. The Gray Man has no eyes, no nose, no mouth.

3   The Gray Man has been seen walking in the surf on the edge of Pawley's Island. He has also been spotted sitting on top of a sand dune staring out to sea, and wandering among swimmers and sunbathers on the beach. But islanders claim that whenever someone has given him a second look, he has instantly vanished.

4   Who is the Gray Man, and why does he appear on Pawley's Island? According to the islanders, the Gray Man materializes only before bad storms. His appearance gives warning of the storm. Islanders do not take those warnings lightly. They

Hurricane Hazel roared up the Eastern Seaboard in October 1954. The Gray Man appeared on Pawley's Island just before Hazel hit.

swear he has yet to be wrong. What is more, they say, whoever sees the Gray Man is spared by the storm.

5   Little Mary McLendon was one of those lucky people. Mary first visited Pawley's Island when she was nine years old. She stayed with her grandmother, who had a house there. A few days before the end of her vacation, Mary took a long walk along the beach. It was late afternoon. Suddenly, ahead of her on a dune, she saw a figure that she recognized as the Gray Man. As she ran to catch up to him, he grew dim and faded away. Mary turned and scurried to her grandmother's house.

6   "Granny! Granny!" she cried, "I have seen the Gray Man. There will be a storm! We must leave the island! Quick, Granny, hurry!"

7   At the same time, a neighbor rushed up to say that a hurricane was indeed on the way. Mary and her grandmother quickly packed and left the island for the town of Georgetown, where Mrs. McLendon had another home.

8   That night the storm struck Pawley's. It dumped several inches of rain and swept over the island with a terrible destruction. In the calm that followed, Mary and her grandmother returned. Everywhere, it seemed, houses had been swept away and palm trees uprooted. Except at the McLendons'. Their property was untouched. A doll's suitcase Mary had forgotten on the front step was still there. Clothes that had been hung on a line remained neatly in place. It was as if a giant protective bubble had been lowered over the house while the storm raged all around.

9   Other islanders have had similar experiences. It's no wonder, then, that they insist that the Gray Man exists. But who was, or is, he? There are several theories.

10   Some folks think he is the ghost of Percival Pawley, the first settler of Pawley's Island. Others, however, claim he is the ghost of a young man who lived in the 18th century—a man who was to have married the daughter of a rich plantation owner.

Homes along the ocean on Pawley's Island, South Carolina

11   The man and woman, it was said, were cousins. They had been separated for two years when the young man was killed in a duel in Europe. Hearing of his death, his fiancée retreated to her room, vowing to stay there until her own life should end.

12   Then one day an old friend paid her a call. He had recently lost his wife, so the two had something in common to talk about. Their conversations led to a renewed friendship, and eventually to love and marriage. The couple went to live in Charleston, South Carolina. They also kept a home on Pawley's Island, where they spent the summers.

13   Then came the summer of 1778. It was the midst of the American Revolution. The woman went to live on Pawley's while her husband fought the British. Late in the summer, a hurricane struck. Fortunately for the young woman, her home was unharmed. In the calm after the storm, a survivor from a shipwreck knocked at her door, seeking help. When the woman opened the door, whom should she see standing there but the cousin who had supposedly been killed in a duel! She fainted with shock, and the shipwrecked man fled. He was found on the mainland a few days later, dead of some kind of fever.

14   After the revolution, the woman and her husband were reunited. They continued to spend summers on Pawley's. But wherever she was on the island, the woman was haunted by a shadowy figure that followed her at a distance. She was

sure it was the ghost of her cousin.

15   Within months, other residents of the island began to talk of a gray figure that appeared just before storms. Over the years that followed, he appeared before all of the fiercest storms. The Gray Man was seen just before the great storms of 1822, 1893, and 1916 shattered the island. He was seen again in 1954, just before Hurricane Hazel hit. And he was there again a year later, when Hurricane Connie devastated the entire Carolina coast.

16   Each time, all who saw him, and all who believed the warnings of those people, had ample time to leave the island. Their lives were spared. To learn the fate of those who either didn't see the Gray Man or didn't believe in his warnings, you have only to look at photographs of the awful destruction on Pawley's Island after those storms.

If you have been timed while reading this article, enter your reading time below. Then turn to the Words-per-Minute Table on page 71 and look up your reading speed (words per minute). Enter your reading speed on the graph on page 72.

Reading Time: Lesson 2

_____ : _____
Minutes   Seconds

A | **Finding the Main Idea**

One statement below expresses the main idea of the article. One statement is too general, or too broad. The other statement explains only part of the article; it is too narrow. Label the statements using the following key:

M—Main Idea   **B—Too Broad**   **N—Too Narrow**

_____ 1. A ghost called the Gray Man is said to appear on Pawley's Island, South Carolina, to warn people of approaching storms.

_____ 2. The ghostly Gray Man of Pawley's Island has no face.

_____ 3. Pawley's Island, South Carolina, has a resident ghost that helps the islanders.

_____ Score 15 points for a correct M answer.

_____ Score 5 points for each correct B or N answer.

_____ **Total Score:** Finding the Main Idea

 B | **Recalling Facts**

How well do you remember the facts in the article? Put an X in the box next to the answer that correctly completes each statement about the article.

1. The Gray Man
   ☐ a.   never appears in winter.
   ☐ b.   has no face.
   ☐ c.   is the ghost of a British soldier.

2. When Mary McLendon saw the Gray Man, she
   ☐ a.   had just settled on the island.
   ☐ b.   was sick with a fever.
   ☐ c.   was nine years old.

3. The plantation owner's daughter was told her cousin was killed in
   ☐ a.   the Revolutionary War.
   ☐ b.   a duel.
   ☐ c.   a storm at sea.

4. According to the story, the Gray Man has been around for
   ☐ a.   just over two hundred years.
   ☐ b.   about a hundred years.
   ☐ c.   almost four hundred years.

5. The Gray Man is
   ☐ a.   tall and skinny.
   ☐ b.   short and fat.
   ☐ c.   short and skinny.

Score 5 points for each correct answer.

_____ **Total Score:** Recalling Facts

C Making Inferences

When you combine your own experience and information from a text to draw a conclusion that is not directly stated in that text, you are making an inference. Below are five statements that may or may not be inferences based on information in the article. Label the statements using the following key:

C—Correct Inference   **F—Faulty Inference**

_____ 1. The Gray Man has never spoken to anyone.

_____ 2. Pawley's Island is a summer vacation spot.

_____ 3. The Gray Man has not been seen since Hurricane Connie in 1955.

_____ 4. Mary McLendon was frightened at the sight of the Gray Man.

_____ 5. The residents of Pawley's Island like having a ghost around.

Score 5 points for each correct answer.

_____ **Total Score:** Making Inferences

D Using Words Precisely

Each numbered sentence below contains an underlined word or phrase from the article. Following the sentence are three definitions. One definition is closest to the meaning of the underlined word. One definition is opposite or nearly opposite. Label those two definitions using the following key. Do not label the remaining definition.

C—Closest   **O—Opposite or Nearly Opposite**

1. He does have one <u>remarkable</u> feature.

_____ a. extraordinary

_____ b. common

_____ c. ugly

2. According to the islanders, the Gray Man <u>materializes</u> only before bad storms.

_____ a. speaks

_____ b. vanishes

_____ c. appears

3. Their conversations led to a <u>renewed</u> friendship, and eventually to love and marriage.

_____ a. reestablished

_____ b. secret

_____ c. ended

4. Each time, all who saw him, and all who believed the warnings of those people, had <u>ample</u> time to leave the island.

_____ a. lost

_____ b. plenty

_____ c. too little

5. To learn the <u>fate</u> of those who didn't believe in the warnings, you have only to look at photographs of the awful destruction on Pawley's Island after those storms.

_____ a. final outcome

_____ b. beginning condition

_____ c. news

_____ Score 3 points for each correct C answer.

_____ Score 2 points for each correct O answer.

_____ **Total Score:** Using Words Precisely

Enter the four total scores in the spaces below, and add them together to find your Reading Comprehension Score. Then record your score on the graph on page 73.

Score	Question Type	Lesson 2
_____	Finding the Main Idea	
_____	Recalling Facts	
_____	Making Inferences	
_____	Using Words Precisely	
_____	**Reading Comprehension Score**	

Author's Approach

Put an X in the box next to the correct answer.

1. The author uses the first sentence of the article to

☐ a. entertain the reader with a ghost story.

☐ b. describe qualities of the Gray Man.

☐ c. compare the Gray Man to other ghosts on Pawley's Island.

2. What does the author mean by the statement "The Gray Man hardly looks like a champion, however"?

☐ a. The Gray Man doesn't look like a typical hero.

☐ b. The Gray Man hasn't won any awards.

☐ c. The Gray Man looks sickly.

3. What is the author's purpose in writing "The Gray Man of Pawley's Island"?

☐ a. To convey a light-hearted mood

☐ b. To inform the reader about the mysterious ghost of Pawley's Island

☐ c. To warn the reader to avoid the Gray Man

4. How is the author's purpose for writing the article expressed in paragraph 10?

☐ a. The author relates two theories that explain the Gray Man's identity.

☐ b. The author tries to convince the reader that the Gray Man is the ghost of a young man who lived in the 18th century.

☐ c. The author creates a fearful mood by describing the Gray Man.

_____ Number of correct answers

Record your personal assessment of your work on the Critical Thinking Chart on page 74.

CRITICAL THINKING

Summarizing and Paraphrasing

Follow the directions provided for question 1. Put an X in the box next to the correct answer for question 2.

1. Reread paragraph 13 in the article. Below, write a summary of the paragraph in no more than 25 words.

_____

_____

_____

Reread your summary and decide whether it covers the important ideas in the paragraph. Next, try to shorten the summary to 15 words or less without leaving out any essential information. Write this summary below.

_____

_____

_____

2. Choose the best one-sentence paraphrase for the following sentence from the article:

"Hearing of his death, his fiancée retreated to her room, vowing to stay there until her own life should end."

☐ a. After his death, the man's fiancée went to her room and stayed there until she died.

☐ b. After hearing about his death, the man's fiancée tried to kill herself.

☐ c. After she heard about his death, the man's fiancée swore she'd stay in her room until she died.

_____ Number of correct answers

Record your personal assessment of your work on the Critical Thinking Chart on page 74.

Critical Thinking

Put an X in the box next to the correct answer for questions 1 and 2. Follow the directions provided for the other questions.

1. Which of the following statements from the article is an opinion rather than a fact?

☐ a. "Mary first visited Pawley's Island when she was nine years old."

☐ b. "[The storm] dumped several inches of rain and swept the island with a terrible destruction."

☐ c. "The Gray Man hardly looks like a champion, however."

2. From what the article told about the Gray Man, you can predict that

☐ a. he will appear again just before another bad storm hits Pawley's Island.

☐ b. people will run away in fear when they see him.

☐ c. he will leave Pawley's to haunt another island.

3. Choose from the letters below to correctly complete the following statement. Write the letters on the lines.

On the positive side, _____, but on the negative side _____.

a. when you see the Gray Man, it means that a very bad storm is coming

b. the Gray Man dresses in a gray suit with a long jacket

c. the Gray Man's appearances have saved many lives

4. Choose from the letters below to correctly complete the following statement. Write the letters on the lines.

According to the article, _____ caused Mary McLendon to _____, and the effect was _____.

   a. tell her grandmother that a storm was coming

   b. Mary and her grandmother quickly left the island

   c. the appearance of the Gray Man

5. Which paragraphs from the article provide evidence that supports your answer to question 4?

_____

_____ Number of correct answers

Record your personal assessment of your work on the Critical Thinking Chart on page 74.

Personal Response

How do you think you would feel if you saw the Gray Man?

_____

_____

_____

I wonder why

_____

_____

_____

_____

Self-Assessment

When reading the article, I was having trouble with

_____

_____

_____

_____

CRITICAL THINKING

STRANGE HAPPENINGS AT THE HARVARD EXIT THEATER

In the early part of the 20th century, the building that now houses the Harvard Exit Theater was the home of the Woman's Century Club.

In most theaters, the only ghosts are the ones on the screen. But that's not the case at the Harvard Exit Theater. Ever since this movie house opened in 1968, ghostly figures have been making their presence felt.

2   The Harvard Exit Theater has nothing to do with Harvard University. The theater is located in Seattle, Washington. Its name comes from a local highway exit. The movie house is a stately old three-story building with lots of charm. There is a fireplace in the parlor and antiques in the lobby. The building once served as a meeting place. In the early 1900s, women gathered there to lobby for voting rights. Later, the building became home to a women's civic group. In 1968, film projectors and movie screens were installed, and the place became a movie house.

3   At first, the Harvard Exit Theater seemed normal enough. People came to view foreign films and old classics. Soon, though, strange things began to happen. Manager Janet Wainwright was the first to notice them. One morning Wainwright

unlocked the theater as usual. To her surprise, she found a fire already burning in the fireplace. On another day, she found that the furniture in the lobby had been moved. Some mornings the chairs were drawn into a circle. Other days the lights were on. And once Wainwright walked into the theater and saw a woman sitting there reading a book.

4   As Wainwright stared at the woman, she realized the figure could not be a living person. Wainwright could see right through her. The figure turned, looked at Wainwright, and smiled. Then she—or it—closed the book, turned off the lamp, and walked out of the room.

5   Janet Wainwright was not the only one to have bizarre experiences at the theater. One employee heard the sound of a woman sobbing. Another found that the film projector had been turned on while the theater was empty. And several other employees saw a transparent figure like the one Wainwright had seen. The woman was always dressed in clothing that seemed to date from the early 1900s.

6   By 1982, Janet Wainwright had left her job at the theater. A new manager had taken over. His name was Alan Blangy, and he made it clear that he did not believe in ghosts. Soon, though, Blangy had to rethink his beliefs.

7   "I was closing the theater one night," said Blangy, "and I heard people in the auditorium on the third floor. We had been closed for a while, and I thought they must be just sitting there talking." Blangy went up to check it out. He found the third floor deserted. As he entered the auditorium, however, he heard the fire exit door open and close.

8   "I went over to make sure it had closed tightly. It hadn't but when I pulled on the panic bar there was someone on the other side tugging back. I kept pulling and pulling." Finally Blangy got the door closed. By that time, his assistant had come to see what was going on. The two of them knew that whoever had been pulling on the door was still there. The only way to the street was down the noisy metal fire escape. They hadn't heard anyone clambering down those stairs, so they knew the person or persons had not gone away. "We opened the door together," Blangy recalled. "There was nobody there…. It was real spooky."

9   Meanwhile, other employees continued to come face to face with a ghostly figure. One woman was working alone in an office on the second floor late one night. When she walked out into the hallway, she began to scream. A pale woman was hovering in the air at the other end of the hall.

10   Alice McCullough also came across a ghost at the theater. "One night about half an hour after I got there, I was

Bertha Landes, the only woman ever to serve as mayor of Seattle, Washington, now spends her time with other ghosts haunting the Harvard Exit Theater in Seattle.

vacuuming and it was real loud and I had the radio on, and I got this sense that someone else was in the building with me," McCullough reported. "I turned off the vacuum and turned around, and I saw this figure with an old-fashioned dress, real transparent. It didn't last very long, but then I didn't stay there very long either. I looked away from it and left the auditorium."

11   In 1985, investigators came to the Harvard Exit Theater. They wanted to check out the strange happenings. The group was made up of psychics and others who had done research on hauntings. Blangy agreed to let them spend several nights in the theater.

12   The group set up tape recorders in the building. The tapes picked up a number of strange noises. Meanwhile, a magnet placed in one doorway spun wildly. It was as though some unseen person were twirling it around. Also, a ball of energy was detected on the third floor. It moved through the auditorium. Then it went out the fire exit where Blangy's tug-of-war had taken place.

13   Still, no one knew how many ghosts were in the theater. No one knew who they were or why they were haunting the building. Local TV stations brought in more psychics to help answer these questions. The psychics said they made contact with several ghosts. Some were the spirits of women who had used the building for meetings at the turn of the century. One was Bertha Landis, the only woman ever to serve as mayor of Seattle. Another ghost was a man named Peter who died on the site where the present building was built.

14   No one is sure who the ghosts really are, or why they frequent the Harvard Exit Theater. Luckily, the spirits don't seem angry or violent. Still, it is unnerving to know that at any moment a ghost may appear from nowhere…and then disappear again into thin air.

If you have been timed while reading this article, enter your reading time below. Then turn to the Words-per-Minute Table on page 71 and look up your reading speed (words per minute). Enter your reading speed on the graph on page 72.

Reading Time: **Lesson 3**

_____ : _____
Minutes   Seconds

Finding the Main Idea

One statement below expresses the main idea of the article. One statement is too general, or too broad. The other statement explains only part of the article; it is too narrow. Label the statements using the following key:

M—Main Idea   **B—Too Broad**   **N—Too Narrow**

_____ 1. Some employees at the Harvard Exit Theater saw a transparent female figure dressed in clothing dating from the early 1900s.

_____ 2. For many years, strange things happened in a Seattle theater.

_____ 3. Since 1968, employees at the Harvard Exit Theater in Seattle have heard strange noises and seen ghostly figures in the building.

_____ Score 15 points for a correct M answer.

_____ Score 5 points for each correct B or N answer.

_____ **Total Score:** Finding the Main Idea

 Recalling Facts

How well do you remember the facts in the article? Put an X in the box next to the answer that correctly completes each statement about the article.

1. The Harvard Exit Theater is located
    ☐ a. at Harvard University.
    ☐ b. in Seattle, Washington.
    ☐ c. on the highway.

2. The transparent figure that Wainwright saw in the theater
    ☐ a. was dressed in clothing from the early 1900s.
    ☐ b. was sobbing.
    ☐ c. turned on the film projector.

3. When Alan Blangy and his assistant opened the fire exit door,
    ☐ a. they saw a pale woman hovering in the air.
    ☐ b. no one was there.
    ☐ c. someone ran noisily down the metal fire escape.

4. In 1985, the theater was investigated by
    ☐ a. local TV stations.
    ☐ b. Bertha Landis.
    ☐ c. a group of psychics.

5. Tape recorders set up in the building
    ☐ a. moved through the auditorium.
    ☐ b. spun wildly in a doorway.
    ☐ c. picked up lots of strange noises.

Score 5 points for each correct answer.

_____ **Total Score:** Recalling Facts

C | Making Inferences

When you combine your own experience and information from a text to draw a conclusion that is not directly stated in that text, you are making an inference. Below are five statements that may or may not be inferences based on information in the article. Label the statements using the following key:

C—Correct Inference   **F—Faulty Inference**

_____ 1. Janet Wainwright left her job at the theater because she was afraid of the ghosts that haunted the building.

_____ 2. Alice McCullough cleaned the theater.

_____ 3. The ghosts in the theater wanted to scare everyone away from the theater.

_____ 4. Some psychics claim that they can communicate with the spirits of the dead.

_____ 5. Spirits hang around the Harvard Exit Theater because they like to watch foreign films and old classics.

Score 5 points for each correct answer.

_____ **Total Score:** Making Inferences

D | Using Words Precisely

Each numbered sentence below contains an underlined word or phrase from the article. Following the sentence are three definitions. One definition is closest to the meaning of the underlined word. One definition is opposite or nearly opposite. Label those two definitions using the following key. Do not label the remaining definition.

C—Closest   **O—Opposite or Nearly Opposite**

1. The movie house is a <u>stately</u> old three-story building with lots of charm.

_____ a. publicly owned

_____ b. dignified and impressive

_____ c. shabby

2. And several other employees saw a <u>transparent</u> figure like the one Wainwright had seen.

_____ a. solid

_____ b. old-fashioned

_____ c. see-through

3. They hadn't heard anyone <u>clambering</u> down those stairs, so they knew the person or persons had not gone away.

_____ a. scrambling awkwardly

_____ b. walking slowly and carefully

_____ c. singing

4. No one is sure who the ghosts really are, or why they <u>frequent</u> the Harvard Exit Theater.

_____ a. like

_____ b. avoid

_____ c. hang around

5. Still, it is <u>unnerving</u> to know that at any moment a ghost may appear from nowhere…and then disappear again into thin air.

_____ a. upsetting

_____ b. reassuring

_____ c. incredible

_____ Score 3 points for each correct C answer.

_____ Score 2 points for each correct O answer.

_____ **Total Score:** Using Words Precisely

Enter the four total scores in the spaces below, and add them together to find your Reading Comprehension Score. Then record your score on the graph on page 73.

Score	Question Type	Lesson 3
_____	Finding the Main Idea	
_____	Recalling Facts	
_____	Making Inferences	
_____	Using Words Precisely	
_____	**Reading Comprehension Score**	

Author's Approach

Put an X in the box next to the correct answer.

1. The main purpose of the first paragraph is to

☐ a. compare the ghosts in the Harvard Exit Theater with those on screen.

☐ b. inform the reader that ghosts inhabit the Harvard Exit Theater.

☐ c. encourage the reader to believe in ghosts.

2. From the statements below, choose those that you believe the author would agree with.

☐ a. The spirits that inhabit the theater do not want to harm anyone.

☐ b. The employees at the theater just imagined the strange sights and sounds they reported.

☐ c. People in Seattle were interested in hearing about the strange occurrences in the theater.

3. The author tells this story mainly by

☐ a. retelling Janet Wainwright's experiences with the ghosts.

☐ b. comparing the ghosts in the Harvard Exit Theater with those in other buildings.

☐ c. telling different people's experiences with the ghosts that haunt the Harvard Exit Theater.

_____ Number of correct answers

Record your personal assessment of your work on the Critical Thinking Chart on page 74.

CRITICAL THINKING

Summarizing and Paraphrasing

Put an X in the box next to the correct answer for questions 1 and 3. Follow the directions provided for question 2.

1. Below are summaries of the article. Choose the summary that says all the most important things about the article but in the fewest words.

☐ a. After employees had reported seeing and hearing ghosts in the Harvard Exit Theater for many years, psychics came to investigate the strange happenings.

☐ b. Psychics discovered that some of the ghosts were the spirits of women who had used the building in the early 1900s.

☐ c. Employees at the Harvard Exit Theater reported seeing ghosts in the building. They also heard strange noises. In 1985, psychics contacted several of the ghosts. Some of these ghosts, they claimed, were the spirits of women who had used the building in the early 1900s.

2. Reread paragraph 8 in the article. Below, write a summary of the paragraph in no more than 25 words.

_____

_____

_____

_____

Reread your summary and decide whether it covers the important ideas in the paragraph. Next, try to shorten the summary to about 15 words or less without leaving out any essential information. Write this summary below.

_____

_____

3. Read the statement about the article below. Then read the paraphrase of that statement. Choose the reason that best tells why the paraphrase does not say the same thing as the statement.

Statement: The people who worked at the theater never knew when they would see a ghostly figure dressed in old-fashioned clothing or hovering in the air.

Paraphrase: At random times, employees at the theater saw the transparent figures of women dressed in turn-of-the-century clothing or women who floated in the air and then disappeared.

☐ a. Paraphrase says too much.

☐ b. Paraphrase doesn't say enough.

☐ c. Paraphrase doesn't agree with the statement about the article.

_____ Number of correct answers

Record your personal assessment of your work on the Critical Thinking Chart on page 74.

Critical Thinking

Put an X in the box next to the correct answer for questions 1, 2, and 4. Follow the directions provided for questions 3 and 5.

1. Which of the following statements from the article is an opinion rather than a fact?

☐ a. "The building once served as a meeting place. In the early 1900s, women gathered there to lobby for voting rights."

☐ b. "By 1982, Janet Wainwright had left her job at the theater. A new manager had taken over."

☐ c. "It was real spooky."

2. From the information in paragraph 12, you can predict that

☐ a. the psychics would interpret these findings as evidence that someone was trying to trick them.

☐ b. the ghosts would try to hide from the psychics.

☐ c. the psychics would interpret these findings as evidence that ghosts inhabited the building.

3. Choose from the letters below to correctly complete the following statement. Write the letters on the lines.

In the article, _____ and _____ are alike.

a. the ghost that Alan Blangy saw

b. the ghost that Alice McCullough saw

c. the ghost that Janet Wainwright saw

4. What was the cause of a woman's screaming when she walked out into the hallway of the theater late one night?

☐ a. She was working alone.

☐ b. She saw a pale woman hovering in the air.

☐ c. She found a fire burning in the fireplace.

5. In which paragraph did you find the information or details to answer question 4?

_____

_____ Number of correct answers

Record your personal assessment of your work on the Critical Thinking Chart on page 74.

Personal Response

Begin the first 5–8 sentences of your own article about a public building that you think could be haunted. It may tell of a real experience or one that is imagined.

_____

_____

_____

_____

Self-Assessment

I'm proud of how I answered question # _____ in section _____ because

_____

_____

_____

CRITICAL THINKING

THE GHOSTS OF FLIGHT 401

It was mid-December 1972. Eastern Airlines flight attendant Doris Elliot was working a flight from New York to Florida when she suddenly got what she later described as a "weird, sick feeling." In her mind she saw a vision of an Eastern jet flying at night over the Florida Everglades. The left wing of that plane suddenly crumpled, and the jet hurtled into the swamp. Screams pierced the night.

2   White as a sheet, Doris fell into a seat. Two other attendants asked her what was wrong. Doris told them what she had "seen." It was not her first experience with such visions. She had often had mental pictures of events that later took place in real life.

3   The two attendants were shaken. They had faith in Doris's premonitions. "When is the plane going to crash?" they asked.

4   "Close to New Year's," Doris answered.

5   "Is it going to be us?"

6   "No," Doris said, "but it's going to be real close."

7   At 7:30 P.M. on Friday, December 29, 1972, one of Eastern's new Tristar jets, the L-1011, landed in New York. It had come from Miami and would make a short

Eastern Airlines Flight 401 was a Lockheed L-1011. This is a view of the cockpit of an L-1011.

layover before flying back. The entire cockpit crew—Captain Bob Loft, First Officer Bert Stockstill, and Second Officer Don Repo—had volunteered for Flight 401. The short round-trip flight would put them home in Miami with their families for the holiday.

8   Captain Loft looked at his watch. A cabin crew was flying up from Miami to work the flight. But they were late, so a last-minute change was planned. The same cabin crew that had flown with the plane into New York would remain aboard. Among the crew was Doris Elliot.

9   Then, at 8:40 P.M., the scheduled cabin crew landed in New York. They rushed onto Flight 401. Doris Elliot and the others got off.

10   Flight 401 took off at 9:20 P.M., and both passengers and crew were in a holiday mood. By 11:30, Captain Loft had his landing instructions from Miami. Soon he gave the order to lower the landing gear. As the gear descended, a warning light flashed. Something seemed to be wrong with the nosewheel. Loft began to circle, and he set the automatic pilot, while the cockpit crew checked out the problem.

11   Within a minute the giant jet began to lose altitude. The automatic pilot had somehow disengaged. The crew was so busy looking into the problem indicated by the warning light for the nosewheel that no one noticed the altimeter dropping, and in the black of night there were no visual signs that the plane was descending. The flight recorder later revealed Captain Loft's words as the earth suddenly loomed close in the light of the plane. "What's going on here?" he cried. The next instant Flight 401 crashed into the Everglades, killing 161 people, including the entire cockpit crew. Doris Elliot's vision had come true.

12   Four months after the disaster, in the spring of 1973, flight attendant Ginny Packard was working another Flight 401—also an L-1011—from New York to Miami. While she was in the galley preparing meals, a cloud about the size of a grapefruit appeared in front of her. Dumbfounded, she watched as the cloud formed a human face.

13   Ginny ran from the galley. Was she going crazy? She didn't think so. But who would believe she had just seen the ghost of Second Officer Don Repo?

14   A few weeks later, that same L-1011 was at Newark Airport in New Jersey, preparing to take off. When senior flight attendant Sis Patterson took a routine head count of passengers in the first-class section, she noticed an extra passenger—a man dressed in the uniform of an Eastern Airlines captain.

15   "Excuse me, Captain," she said. "I don't have you on my passenger list." The man stared straight ahead, as if he had not heard a word. "Sir," she repeated, "may I have your name?" Still no answer.

The rear jet engine and part of the tail assembly of Eastern Airlines Flight 401 after it crashed in the Florida Everglades in 1972

16 A second attendant approached the man and inquired if he was ill. He seemed to be in a daze. That attendant, too, got no response to her questions.

17 The two women called their captain for help. As he leaned over to talk to the man, his face registered shock and disbelief. "It's Bob Loft!" he announced. No one moved. There was total silence. Then the uniformed figure vanished. One moment he was there; the next he wasn't!

18 A number of other strange occurrences involving the crew of the ill-fated Flight 401 also took place on L-1011s. On at least five other occasions, either Captain Loft or Second Officer Repo materialized on the jets.

19 It was reported that Don Repo told one crew, "There will never be another crash of an L-1011. We will not let it happen." He is said to have warned another crew, "Watch out for fire on this airplane." Shortly thereafter, an engine caught fire. The crew was able to land the disabled plane safely.

20 Had ghosts actually appeared on those Eastern flights? The airline wasn't talking —for obvious reasons. Neither were most of the flight crews, who were afraid they would be fired if they spoke out. Then John Fuller entered the picture.

21 A well-respected science writer, Fuller, by his own admission, did not believe in ghosts. But he was a curious person. He was determined to get to the bottom of the mystery.

22 After months of coaxing the flight crews who had witnessed the incidents, he was able to get some people to tell their stories. Even then, they made him swear that he would never reveal their names. Fuller kept that promise.

23 The interviews convinced Fuller that he could not shrug off the incidents. Too many people, who had too much to lose to make up stories, claimed to have seen the ghosts. Still, Fuller wanted hard evidence of the ghosts' existence.

24 He tried mediums—people who claim to be able to contact the spirit world—but nothing they came up with convinced him. Then he decided to try using a Ouija board to reach the spirit of Don Repo. A Ouija board is a board on which are printed the letters of the alphabet, the numerals one to nine and zero, and the words yes and no. Users rest their fingertips lightly on a flat triangular marker and concentrate on the spirit they wish to contact. The marker will supposedly move around the board to the markings, spelling out messages from the spirit.

25 Using a Ouija board, Fuller got a lot of information about the plane crash. But none of it was the kind of hard evidence he demanded. Then he got two more messages—gibberish, or so he thought: *Did the mice leave that family closet?* and *To go into wastebasket pennies sit there boys room.* What could those messages mean? Fuller telephoned Repo's wife.

26 "Tell me," he said, "did you ever have mice in what you call your 'family closet'?" Alice Repo was taken by surprise. "How did you know about that?" She explained that some mice had built a nest in the attic above their family room. The only way to get to the attic to set traps was through the family room closet.

27 Next Fuller asked, "Did Don have anything to do with some pennies in a wastebasket in your boy's room?" "This is amazing, " Alice Repo said. "Don used to collect Indian head pennies. There's a small barrel full of them in our son's room."

28 John Fuller was satisfied. Only the Repos could have known those facts. As far as John Fuller was concerned, the ghosts of Flight 401 were indeed real.

29 Note: In accord with the wishes of the flight attendants, their real names have not been used.

If you have been timed while reading this article, enter your reading time below. Then turn to the Words-per-Minute Table on page 71 and look up your reading speed (words per minute). Enter your reading speed on the graph on page 72.

Reading Time: Lesson 4

_____ : _____
Minutes   Seconds

A Finding the Main Idea

One statement below expresses the main idea of the article. One statement is too general, or too broad. The other statement explains only part of the article; it is too narrow. Label the statements using the following key:

M—Main Idea   B—Too Broad   N—Too Narrow

_____ 1. Some people claim to have seen the ghosts of the crew of a jet that crashed.

_____ 2. According to reports of reliable witnesses, ghosts of the crew of a downed Eastern Airlines L-1011 have appeared on a number of other L-1011 flights.

_____ 3. The ghost of Second Officer Don Repo warned one L-1011 crew that there would be a fire on their plane.

_____ Score 15 points for a correct M answer.

_____ Score 5 points for each correct B or N answer.

_____ **Total Score:** Finding the Main Idea

B Recalling Facts

How well do you remember the facts in the article? Put an X in the box next to the answer that correctly completes each statement about the article.

1. Flight 401 traveled regularly between
   ☐ a. New York and Miami.
   ☐ b. Miami and Washington.
   ☐ c. Washington and New York.

2. The captain of the Flight 401 that crashed was
   ☐ a. Bob Loft.
   ☐ b. Bert Stockstill.
   ☐ c. Don Repo.

3. Flight 401 crashed in
   ☐ a. Florida.
   ☐ b. Georgia.
   ☐ c. New York.

4. John Fuller decided to investigate the reports of the ghosts of Flight 401 because he
   ☐ a. made his living as a ghost hunter.
   ☐ b. was hired by Eastern to get to the bottom of things.
   ☐ c. was curious to know the truth.

5. John Fuller persuaded witnesses to talk by
   ☐ a. offering them money for their stories.
   ☐ b. promising to keep their identities secret.
   ☐ c. threatening to report them to their superiors.

Score 5 points for each correct answer.

_____ **Total Score:** Recalling Facts

C Making Inferences

When you combine your own experience and information from a text to draw a conclusion that is not directly stated in that text, you are making an inference. Below are five statements that may or may not be inferences based on information in the article. Label the statements using the following key:

C—Correct Inference   F—Faulty Inference

_____ 1. L-1011s have a poor safety record.

_____ 2. If the captain had been paying attention to the altimeter, the plane might not have crashed.

_____ 3. The ghosts of Flight 401 were trying to keep people from flying on L-1011s.

_____ 4. As a result of John Fuller's investigation, Eastern Airlines stopped using L-1011s.

_____ 5. Eastern Airlines officials felt that the public reports of the ghosts would hurt the airline.

Score 5 points for each correct answer.

_____ **Total Score:** Making Inferences

D Using Words Precisely

Each numbered sentence below contains an underlined word or phrase from the article. Following the sentence are three definitions. One definition is closest to the meaning of the underlined word. One definition is opposite or nearly opposite. Label those two definitions using the following key. Do not label the remaining definition.

C—Closest   O—Opposite or Nearly Opposite

1. The left wing of the plane crumpled, and the jet <u>hurtled</u> into the swamp.

_____ a. lagged behind

_____ b. moved at great speed

_____ c. twirled

2. They had faith in Doris's <u>premonitions</u>.

_____ a. predictions

_____ b. flashbacks

_____ c. prayers

3. The flight recorder later revealed Captain Loft's words as the earth suddenly <u>loomed</u> close in the light of the plane.

_____ a. vanished

_____ b. appeared

_____ c. exploded

4. As he leaned over to talk to the man, his face <u>registered</u> shock and disbelief.

_____ a. photographed

_____ b. hid

_____ c. expressed

5. The crew was able to land the <u>disabled</u> plane safely.

_____ a. crippled

_____ b. commercial

_____ c. undamaged

_____ Score 3 points for each correct C answer.

_____ Score 2 points for each correct O answer.

_____ **Total Score:** Using Words Precisely

Enter the four total scores in the spaces below, and add them together to find your Reading Comprehension Score. Then record your score on the graph on page 73.

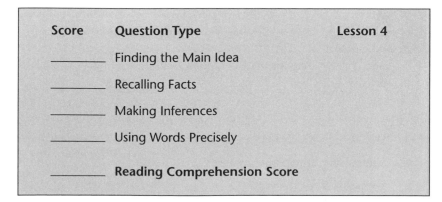

Score	Question Type	Lesson 4
_____	Finding the Main Idea	
_____	Recalling Facts	
_____	Making Inferences	
_____	Using Words Precisely	
_____	**Reading Comprehension Score**	

Author's Approach

Put an X in the box next to the correct answer.

1. The main purpose of the first paragraph is to

☐ a. suggest the possibility that the terrible vision might come true.

☐ b. show that Doris Elliot was mentally unstable and dangerous.

☐ c. prove that working too long can make flight attendants giddy.

2. From the statements below, choose those that you believe the author would agree with.

☐ a. Doris Elliot's premonition of a plane crash came true.

☐ b. The crew members who claim to have seen the ghosts of Loft and Repo are crazy.

☐ c. John Fuller kept an open mind as he conducted his investigation into the Flight 401 mystery.

3. What does the author imply by saying "After months of coaxing the flight crews who had witnessed the incidents, [Fuller] was able to get some people to tell their stories"?

☐ a. The flight crews were eager to talk to Fuller.

☐ b. The flight crews did not want to talk about what they had seen.

☐ c. The flight crews did not like Fuller.

4. The author probably wrote this article in order to

☐ a. persuade the reader to avoid traveling by air.

☐ b. express an opinion about people who believe in ghosts.

☐ c. inform the reader about the mystery surrounding Flight 401.

_____ Number of correct answers

Record your personal assessment of your work on the Critical Thinking Chart on page 74.

CRITICAL THINKING

Summarizing and Paraphrasing

Put an X in the box next to the correct answer.

1. Below are summaries of the article. Choose the summary that says all the most important things about the article but in the fewest words.

☐ a. After a flight attendant had a premonition about a plane crash, her vision came true.

☐ b. After Flight 401 crashed, the ghosts of its captain and second officer appeared to warn crew members on other planes of possible dangers.

☐ c. After Flight 401 crashed on its way from New York to Miami, crew members on other planes claimed that they saw the ghosts of the doomed flight's captain and second officer. The ghosts had materialized to prevent other plane crashes.

2. Choose the sentence that correctly restates the following sentence from the article:

"The crew was so busy looking into the problem indicated by the warning light for the nosewheel that no one noticed the altimeter dropping, and in the black of night there were no visual signs that the plane was descending."

☐ a. The crew was busy dealing with the nosewheel problem, and it was so dark outside that they couldn't read the altimeter.

☐ b. The warning light for the nosewheel indicated a problem. The altimeter was broken, so the crew couldn't tell that the plane was going down.

☐ c. While the crew dealt with the nosewheel problem, no one saw the dropping altimeter. The surrounding darkness hid the fact that the plane was descending.

_____ Number of correct answers

Record your personal assessment of your work on the Critical Thinking Chart on page 74.

Critical Thinking

Follow the directions provided for questions 1 and 3. Put an X in the box next to the correct answer for the other questions.

1. For each statement below, write O if it expresses an opinion and write F if it expresses a fact.

_____ a. You can always rely on a Ouija board if you want to contact a spirit.

_____ b. Only really stubborn or close-minded people would refuse to believe in the ghosts of Flight 401.

_____ c. Repo kept a barrel of pennies in his son's bedroom.

2. From the information in paragraph 28, you can predict that John Fuller will

☐ a. be open-minded if he is asked to investigate another supposed ghostly sighting.

☐ b. never believe in ghosts.

☐ c. avoid researching any more ghost sightings.

3. Choose from the letters below to correctly complete the following statement. Write the letters on the lines.

In the article, _____ and _____ are alike.

a. the cockpit crew on the December 29 flight from Miami to New York

b. the cockpit crew on the mid-December flight from New York to Miami

c. the cockpit crew on the December 29 flight from New York to Miami

4. What was the effect of Don Repo's appearance before Ginny Packard?

☐ a. She went to prepare meals in the galley.

☐ b. She ran from the plane's galley.

☐ c. She went crazy.

5. If you were a pilot, how could you use the information in the article to handle a problem with the aircraft?

☐ a. Have the entire crew concentrate on the problem.

☐ b. Depend on the automatic pilot to guide the plane while you attend to the problem.

☐ c. Attend to the problem but keep an eye on other instrument-panel indicators.

_____ Number of correct answers

Record your personal assessment of your work on the Critical Thinking Chart on page 74.

Self-Assessment

A word or phrase in the article that I do not understand is

_____

_____

_____

_____

Personal Response

What new question do you have about this topic?

_____

_____

_____

_____

CRITICAL THINKING

OCEAN-BORN MARY

Ocean-born Mary started life on an 18th-century English sailing ship as her family sailed to the New World.

In the town of Henniker, New Hampshire, stands a grand old house with a fascinating legend attached to it—a legend that some people would like to kill and others insist on preserving. For generations, stories have circulated of eerie happenings in and around the house. It has been said that lights would sometimes flicker on and off in an upstairs window, when no one was living in the house. The awful groans of a dying man have supposedly been heard in the woodyard behind the house. And now and then at dusk a coach drawn by four horses has reportedly taken shape at the front door. Inside the coach, a tall woman with flaming red hair sits, staring off into the distance. The woman, it is said, is the ghost of Ocean-born Mary, and this was once her house.

2 The story of Ocean-born Mary begins in Londonderry, Ireland, in 1720. A shipload of people was setting sail for a new life in the New World. They were bound for Londonderry, New Hampshire. Among those on board were James Wilson and his wife, Elizabeth, who was soon to bear their first child.

3 On July 28, as the voyage was drawing to a close, Elizabeth gave birth to her child. At about the same time, a lookout sighted land—America! Right after, another lookout, perched high atop the mainmast, shouted, "Sail ho!"

4 At that cry, the captain's face remained calm, though inside he was anything but calm. He knew that his ship was easy prey for pirates, who were known to sail those waters. As he debated what to do, the strange ship drew nearer and fired a cannon. Then it broke out the skull and crossbones. Two boats were lowered over the side, and a group of fierce-looking men brandishing swords and pistols rowed swiftly to the immigrant ship and clambered onto its deck. At their head was a tall, dark-skinned man called Pedro. "Lash the men together!" he ordered. "Once we get the valuables, we'll kill them all!"

5 Pedro himself went below decks. He soon found what he was looking for: chests of silver, gold, and jewels. As he knelt to run his hands through the treasure, he heard a whimper. He drew his pistol and followed the sound—down the passageway to a locked cabin door. Pedro crashed through the door, pistol at the ready. What he faced was a terrified Elizabeth Wilson, lying in bed, her newborn baby cradled in her arms.

6 Pedro's fierce look disappeared. He lowered his pistol and approached. "Is it a girl?" he asked gently. "Yes," Elizabeth whispered. "Has she been named yet?" Pedro inquired. "No...not yet," came the hesitant reply.

7 Pedro leaned over to get a better look at the child. "My dear," he said to Elizabeth, "if you give this child my mother's name, I swear I will not harm this ship nor any of its passengers." A bewildered Elizabeth nodded yes. "Her name shall be Mary," Pedro said. Then he left the cabin.

8 Back on deck, he shouted a series of commands to his men. "Return the treasure! Release the men! We are leaving this vessel!" The pirates lowered themselves into their boats and pulled away to their own ship.

9 Shortly after, Pedro returned carrying a bundle. He went straight to Elizabeth's cabin. Thrusting the bundle at her, he said, "This is for little Mary's wedding dress." Pedro then left the ship and sailed away. Inside the package, Elizabeth found a bolt of pale green silk embroidered with flowers.

10 The immigrant ship landed safely in Boston. Shortly afterward, James Wilson died, and Elizabeth and her baby daughter went on to Londonderry, where a piece of land awaited them. The story of the tiny child who had saved a ship spread quickly. Everyone began calling her "Ocean-born Mary."

11 The years passed, and Mary grew to be a beautiful bright-eyed, red-haired woman nearly six feet tall. A contemporary described her as being "elegant in her manners, resolute and determined, of strong mind, quick of comprehension, sharp in her conversation with a strong brogue and full of humor." When she

married, she wore a wedding dress of green silk embroidered with flowers.

12 All to this point is true. The facts are of historical record. Here the legend begins.

13 Mary and her husband, James Wallace, lived in Londonderry and had four sons. When the boys were still very young, Mary's husband died. The pirate Pedro had long since retired form the sea, but he had never forgotten the child he had

Mary Wallace, also known as Ocean-born Mary, is buried in Henniker, New Hampshire, behind the Henniker Town Hall.

48

named for his mother. Hearing that Mary was widowed, Pedro decided to help. He went to Henniker, New Hampshire, accompanied by one of his ship's carpenters. Together they built a great house deep in the woods. Then Pedro sought out Mary.

14   Mary was happy to meet the pirate who had given her her name. She had long been curious about him. She found him to be both kindly and generous. "Care for me in my old age," Pedro said to Mary, "and I will see that you and your sons lack nothing." Mary agreed and went to live in Pedro's house. He gave her a coach-and-four to drive, and he made sure her children were well provided for.

15   Then one day Pedro left for the seacoast. When he returned, he was accompanied by a pirate. The two carried a huge chest, which they lugged deep into the woods and buried. When the last shovelful of earth had been thrown, a cry was heard in the night. Pedro returned from the woods alone. His companion was never seen again.

16   Months later, Mary returned from a drive in her coach-and-four to find the house empty. Where was Pedro? She found him behind the house, dead, his heart pierced by a cutlass. Pedro's body was buried under the huge hearthstone in the kitchen of the great house, where he had often said he wished to be placed.

17   The years went by, and one by one, Mary's sons married and left home. Mary stayed on alone in the house Pedro had built for her. She died there in 1814, at the age of 94. According to legend, Mary's ghost regularly visited the house, usually around sunset.

18   In recent years, the legend has distressed the people who live in the house. There is no ghost, they claim. And they wish people would stop bothering them.

19   First of all, the house, which has come to be called the Ocean-born Mary House, was not Mary's at all. It was built by her son Robert. Mary never lived there.

20   Historical records show that Mary did have four sons, but she also had a daughter. And Mary's husband did not die until he was 81 years old. Mary was 71 at the time—hardly the beautiful young widow of the legend. If Pedro had still been alive at that time, he would have been about 100. He never bought any land in Henniker or went looking for Mary Wallace.

21   In 1798, when she was 78 years old, Mary left Londonderry to live with her son William in Henniker—about a mile from Robert's house. She lived there until her death. Mary was buried in the cemetery behind the Henniker Town Hall. A slate headstone marks her grave. On it are inscribed the words "In Memory of Widow Mary Wallace who died Feb. 13, 1814 in the 94th year of her age."

22   How did such a wild legend grow up around her name? It was all part of a moneymaking scheme. In 1917 a man named Louis Roy bought the Robert Wallace house, which had long been vacant and was in bad condition. He moved in with his mother and renovated the house, filling it with valuable antiques. Then he started the story about Mary and Pedro, the ghost, the buried treasure, and the cries in the woodyard. His story grew and grew, and many people began to believe it. Newspapers and magazines spread the story. People began to come from all over. Mr. Roy gave tours of the house for an admission fee. He even rented shovels for 50 cents apiece, so that folks could dig for the buried treasure.

23   Mr. Roy died in 1965, but by that time the legend had taken on a life of its own. The family that bought the house is still plagued by people wanting to see the ghost. Although the story has been proved to be a fake, some folks just refuse to believe the facts. It seems they'd rather cling to the more colorful fiction. A good ghost story dies hard. What would Mary and Pedro say if they knew?

If you have been timed while reading this article, enter your reading time below. Then turn to the Words-per-Minute Table on page 71 and look up your reading speed (words per minute). Enter your reading speed on the graph on page 72.

Reading Time: Lesson 5

_____ : _____
Minutes   Seconds

A | **Finding the Main Idea**

One statement below expresses the main idea of the article. One statement is too general, or too broad. The other statement explains only part of the article; it is too narrow. Label the statements using the following key:

M—Main Idea   **B—Too Broad**   **N—Too Narrow**

_____ 1. The story of Ocean-born Mary has captured people's imaginations for generations.

_____ 2. Ocean-born Mary was born at sea and named by a pirate.

_____ 3. Ocean-born Mary was a real historical figure around whom a fantastic legend was woven.

_____ Score 15 points for a correct M answer.

_____ Score 5 points for each correct B or N answer.

_____ **Total Score:** Finding the Main Idea

B | **Recalling Facts**

How well do you remember the facts in the article? Put an X in the box next to the answer that correctly completes each statement about the article.

1. The story of Ocean-born Mary takes place mainly
   ☐ a. in Ireland.
   ☐ b. in New Hampshire.
   ☐ c. on board a ship.

2. In reality, Mary Wallace lived most of her life in
   ☐ a. Boston, Massachusetts.
   ☐ b. Londonderry, New Hampshire.
   ☐ c. Henniker, New Hampshire.

3. Pedro gave Elizabeth a bundle that contained
   ☐ a. a bolt of cloth.
   ☐ b. the treasure his men had collected.
   ☐ c. his mother's wedding gown.

4. A few years after her husband's death, Ocean-born Mary went to live with
   ☐ a. her son William.
   ☐ b. her son Robert.
   ☐ c. Louis Roy.

5. Ocean-born Mary had
   ☐ a. two sons only.
   ☐ b. four sons and no daughters.
   ☐ c. four sons and a daughter.

   Score 5 points for each correct answer.

   _____ **Total Score:** Recalling Facts

C **Making Inferences**

When you combine your own experience and information from a text to draw a conclusion that is not directly stated in that text, you are making an inference. Below are five statements that may or may not be inferences based on information in the article. Label the statements using the following key:

C—Correct Inference   **F—Faulty Inference**

_____ 1. After Pedro spared the ship on which Mary Wallace was born, he gave up pirating.

_____ 2. The real Mary Wallace did hope that someday she would get to meet Captain Pedro.

_____ 3. Pedro loved his mother.

_____ 4. Mary Wallace actually led a pretty ordinary life.

_____ 5. Mary's son Robert did not want his mother in his house.

Score 5 points for each correct answer.

_____ **Total Score:** Making Inferences

D **Using Words Precisely**

Each numbered sentence below contains an underlined word or phrase from the article. Following the sentence are three definitions. One definition is closest to the meaning of the underlined word. One definition is opposite or nearly opposite. Label those two definitions using the following key. Do not label the remaining definition.

C—Closest   **O—Opposite or Nearly Opposite**

1. Two boats were lowered over the side, and a group of fierce-looking men <u>brandishing</u> swords and pistols rowed swiftly to the immigrant ship.

_____ a. waving

_____ b. sharpening

_____ c. holding still

2. "No...not yet," came the <u>hesitant</u> reply.

_____ a. whispered

_____ b. firm

_____ c. uncertain

3. "Care for me in my old age," Pedro said to Mary, "and I will see that you and your sons <u>lack</u> nothing."

_____ a. have

_____ b. work

_____ c. do without

4. In recent years, the legend has <u>distressed</u> the people who live in the house.

_____ a. upset

_____ b. pleased

_____ c. puzzled

5. The family that bought the house was <u>plagued</u> by people wanting to see the ghost.

_____ a. murdered

_____ b. tormented

_____ c. soothed

_____ Score 3 points for each correct C answer.

_____ Score 2 points for each correct O answer.

_____ **Total Score:** Using Words Precisely

Enter the four total scores in the spaces below, and add them together to find your Reading Comprehension Score. Then record your score on the graph on page 73.

Score	Question Type	Lesson 5
_____	Finding the Main Idea	
_____	Recalling Facts	
_____	Making Inferences	
_____	Using Words Precisely	
_____	**Reading Comprehension Score**	

Author's Approach

Put an X in the box next to the correct answer.

1. The author uses the first sentence of the article to

☐ a. express an opinion about the Ocean-born Mary legend.

☐ b. introduce the debate over the Ocean-born Mary legend.

☐ c. compare the Ocean-born Mary legend to other ghost legends in Henniker, New Hampshire.

2. In this article, "Here the legend begins" means

☐ a. the following story is probably true, but there is no hard evidence to prove it.

☐ b. the story that follows is absolutely true.

☐ c. the story that follows is probably not true.

3. Choose the statement below that best describes the author's position in paragraph 23.

☐ a. The people who live in Mary's house owe Mr. Roy a debt of gratitude.

☐ b. People want to believe a ghost story, even when it's been proved to be fake.

☐ c. The people who insist on believing the legend created by Mr. Roy are stupid.

_____ Number of correct answers

Record your personal assessment of your work on the Critical Thinking Chart on page 74.

Summarizing and Paraphrasing

Follow the directions provided for questions 1 and 2. Put an X in the box next to the correct answer for question 3.

1. Complete the following one-sentence summary of the article using the lettered phrases from the phrase bank below. Write the letters on the lines.

> **Phrase Bank:**
> a. the source of the legend and the effect it has had on some people
> b. the true story of Mary and Pedro
> c. the legend that has been created about Mary and Pedro

The article about Ocean-born Mary begins with _____, goes on to explain _____, and ends with _____.

2. Reread paragraph 21 in the article. Below, write a summary of the paragraph in no more than 25 words.

_____

_____

_____

_____

Reread your summary and decide whether it covers the important ideas in the paragraph. Next, decide how to shorten the summary to 15 words or less without leaving out any essential information. Write this summary below.

_____

_____

3. Read the statement about the article below. Then read the paraphrase of that statement. Choose the reason that best tells why the paraphrase does not say the same thing as the statement.

Statement: According to the legend, Mary Wallace was a beautiful young widow who needed Pedro's help, but according to the facts, Mary was widowed at the age of 71 and never met Pedro.

Paraphrase: Mary and Pedro never actually met.

☐ a. Paraphrase says too much.

☐ b. Paraphrase doesn't say enough.

☐ c. Paraphrase doesn't agree with the statement about the article.

> _____ Number of correct answers
>
> Record your personal assessment of your work on the Critical Thinking Chart on page 74.

Critical Thinking

Follow the directions provided for questions 2 and 5. Put an X in the box next to the correct answer for questions 1, 3, and 4.

1. From what the article told about the legend of Ocean-born Mary, you can predict that

☐ a. people will continue to believe the fake story.

☐ b. everyone will stop believing the fake story.

☐ c. Mary and Pedro will continue to haunt the Robert Wallace house.

2. Choose from the letters below to correctly complete the following statement. Write the letters on the lines.

In the article, _____ and _____ are different.

a. Louis Roy's story of Ocean-born Mary

b. the legend of Ocean-born Mary

c. the true story of Ocean-born Mary

3. What was the cause of Pedro's decision to leave the immigrant ship and its passengers unharmed?

☐ a. Elizabeth Wilson agreed to make Mary a wedding dress of green silk.

☐ b. Mary Wallace agreed to care for Pedro in his old age.

☐ c. Elizabeth Wilson agreed to name her newborn baby Mary.

4. Of the following theme categories, which would this story fit into?

☐ a. Everyone—even a murderous pirate—is basically good.

☐ b. Almost everyone loves a good ghost story.

☐ c. Some people will do anything for money.

5. In which paragraph did you find the information or details to answer question 3?

_____ Number of correct answers

Record your personal assessment of your work on the Critical Thinking Chart on page 74.

Personal Response

I can't believe

Self-Assessment

Which concepts or ideas from the article were difficult to understand?

Which were easy to understand?

CRITICAL THINKING

THE CASE OF THE MISSING SECRETARY

In the early 1900s, when Hester Holt arrived in Denver, Colorado, Denver was still very much a small town. That fact appealed to Hester, who was very much a small-town girl. She wanted to improve her life, and she was sure that Denver was the place to do it. She found a room in a house run by a Mrs. Britton. With her typing skills, Hester had no trouble finding a job as a secretary.

2   From Hester's first day on the job, Mrs. Bell, her employer, was more than satisfied with Hester's work. Hester did everything that was asked of her and more. And when she was sick, which was seldom, she was sure to notify Mrs. Bell. That was why her failure to show up one day without sending word was so strange.

3   Concerned, Mrs. Bell questioned Hester's coworker Stella Dean. "Hester didn't seem sick yesterday, did she, Stella?" "No, she was very cheerful, in fact," Stella replied. "I'm sure she'll be here tomorrow."

4   When Hester did not show up for work the following day, Mrs. Bell decided to send Stella to investigate. "Go check her rooming house to see what you can

C. G. Alford and Co., Inc., was a typical business office of the early 20th century, much like the office in which Hester Holt worked in Denver.

discover," Mrs. Bell ordered. "Perhaps something has happened to her."

5   Stella returned with unsettling news. "Her landlady says that Hester has gone away without telling anyone," reported Stella, bursting into tears.

6   Mrs. Bell found it difficult to believe that Hester would do such a thing. But when she herself talked to Mrs. Britton, it was just as Stella had said. After leaving the office the previous day, Hester had not returned to her room. It was as if she had vanished into thin air.

7   Mrs. Britton did have the address of Hester's sister, which she gave to Mrs. Bell. "Whenever Hester went away, she asked me to forward her mail there," the landlady explained.

8   Hester's sister, however, could shed no light on the matter. She had not heard from Hester in over a month. "But if anyone knows where she is, it's Pete Simpkins," she said.

9   Pete Simpkins, Hester's fiancé, was as mystified by Hester's disappearance as Hester's sister was. "I haven't seen her since the day she left you," Simpkins told Mrs. Bell. He had been in the country that day, he said, supervising the building of a farm. Cycling home, he had seen Hester Holt and Stella Dean riding in a buggy.

10   "Are you sure?" asked Mrs. Bell. "I'll swear to it," said Simpkins. "I did think it was strange, though, since I know that Hester and Stella don't get along." He explained that he had once been engaged to Stella, then had broken it off because of Stella's uncontrollable temper. "Stella was furious when Hester and I started seeing

each other," said Simpkins.

11   The next day Mrs. Bell questioned Stella Dean. "Did you go for a drive with Hester the night she disappeared?" she asked. "The last time I saw Hester was when she left the office," said Stella. Although she did admit that she and Simpkins had once been engaged, Stella denied that she had any animosity toward Hester. "We were always on the best of terms," she insisted.

12   When Hester was still missing the next day, Mrs. Bell called the police. "It's all very mysterious," she told them. "Please do what you can to find her."

13   The police investigation revealed that Simpkins had been telling the truth. Another witness had seen the two girls riding out of town in a buggy on the day Hester disappeared. Hester had rented the buggy from a car dealer, who confirmed that she had driven off in it alone. The buggy was returned that evening, when the dealer's wife was on duty. She took payment from a woman, but she could not describe her. It had been dark, and the woman had been bundled against the cold.

14   Where was Stella Dean that evening? Her mother claimed that Stella had come home from the office and stayed home all night.

15   Another witness confused the issue by stating that she had seen Hester Holt entering Mrs. Britton's rooming house on the night in question.

16   Although they suspected foul play, the police were forced to drop the case for lack of evidence. Mrs. Bell gave up hoping

that Hester would return and hired a replacement, whose name was Vera Cummings.

17   On her first day in the office, Vera sat in Hester Holt's chair, next to Stella Dean. She soon began to shiver. "Why is it that I start shivering whenever I sit next to you, Stella?" Vera asked. "It must be your imagination," replied Stella.

18   But Vera was so uncomfortable that she moved several feet away. Some time later she remarked, "My, Stella, you

Looking north on Denver's Seventeenth Street in 1896, about the time Hester Holt arrived in town

certainly have long legs!" "What on earth do you mean?" demanded Stella. "Your feet keep kicking mine under the table." "You're imagining things again," Stella snapped. But Vera couldn't help noticing that Stella turned very pale.

19 Three days later, when Vera and Stella were taking a break, Vera asked, "Stella, who is that tall, good-looking woman I've seen following you into the building? I've watched her stand behind you in the elevator, but then she disappears. Does she work in another office?" A frightened look came over Stella's face, but she denied having seen the woman Vera described. "You were dreaming," she said.

20 Mrs. Bell had overheard the conversation, and her interest was aroused. "Can you describe the woman, Vera?" she asked. Mrs. Bell's eyes grew wide as Vera gave a detailed description of a woman who looked exactly like Hester Holt.

21 The next morning the three women arrived at the office at the same time. As they stood outside the door, they heard the sound of typing. "Maybe Hester has come back!" said Mrs. Bell hopefully. Stella remained quiet, but she looked strangely frightened.

22 When they entered the room, the three women stopped in their tracks. The typewriter was indeed typing away, but there was no one there. The room was completely empty!

23 Complaining of a headache, Stella left work early. She stayed out for several weeks. When she finally returned to the office, Pete Simpkins met her at the door, a huge smile on his face. "She never told me, but

she's back!" he exclaimed. "What are you talking about, Pete?" asked Stella crossly.

24 "I'm talking about Hester," Pete answered excitedly. "I just saw her walk into the building." Without saying a word, Stella whirled and ran through the door. Vera Cummings, who had also been about to enter the building, had watched Stella's reaction with interest. "Pete," she asked, "are you sure it was Hester you saw?" "Absolutely," Pete insisted. Then he described the woman he had seen. "Why, that sounds just like the woman I've seen following Stella!" Vera exclaimed. "This is all very strange."

25 The day after Stella's return, things got even stranger. Since Mrs. Bell was out sick, Vera and Stella were alone in the office. At one point Vera glanced at Stella and saw that she had a horrified look on her face. She was staring at a briefcase, which was rocking back and forth for no apparent reason. On the briefcase were the initials H. H.

26 Later the two women were leaving for lunch when Vera, startled by a sharp cry, turned to see Stella staring into a mirror. Stella's own reflection stared back at her. But behind her shoulder was another face, pale and with dark, piercing eyes. It was the face of the woman Vera had seen following Stella—the face, Vera was sure, of Hester Holt.

27 Stella ran from the room, the door slamming behind her. When Vera tried to follow, the door would not open, though she used all her strength. Perplexed, Vera was trying to decide what to do when the door suddenly swung open by itself. On

the other side of the door, Stella Dean lay sprawled on the floor.

28 The police report listed the cause of death as accidental. According to Stella's mother, her daughter had suffered from a bad heart. Only Vera knew that Stella had died of fright.

29 Stella Dean was known for her bad temper. Had it finally gotten the best of her? Had she murdered her rival, Hester Holt, in a fit of jealous rage, and then buried the body by the side of the road on the night Pete Simpkins had seen the two women in the buggy? If so, had the ghost of Hester Holt gotten her revenge? The police report had no answers.

30 Nor did the strange story end with Stella's death. When Vera Cummings returned to work, she saw two women entering the office. One was Stella Dean, who looked just as she had in life, except that she was obviously in terror. The other woman followed close behind her. There was no mistaking the tall, slender figure of Hester Holt. 🍃

If you have been timed while reading this article, enter your reading time below. Then turn to the Words-per-Minute Table on page 71 and look up your reading speed (words per minute). Enter your reading speed on the graph on page 72.

Reading Time: Lesson 6

_____ : _____

Minutes   Seconds

Finding the Main Idea

One statement below expresses the main idea of the article. One statement is too general, or too broad. The other statement explains only part of the article; it is too narrow. Label the statements using the following key:

M—Main Idea   **B—Too Broad**   **N—Too Narrow**

_____ 1. A secretary who had mysteriously disappeared haunted the office where she had worked, finally frightening to death her coworker and possible murderer.

_____ 2. Stella Dean was suspected of murdering her coworker, Hester Holt, in a fit of jealousy.

_____ 3. The mysterious disappearance of a young woman and the sudden, unexplained death of her coworker in the early 1900s left those close to the events wondering if ghosts and foul play were involved.

_____ Score 15 points for a correct M answer.

_____ Score 5 points for each correct B or N answer.

_____ **Total Score:** Finding the Main Idea

 Recalling Facts

How well do you remember the facts in the article? Put an X in the box next to the answer that correctly completes each statement about the article.

1. This story took place in
   ☐ a. Sacramento, California.
   ☐ b. Denver, Colorado.
   ☐ c. Portland, Oregon.

2. Mrs. Bell was Hester Holt's
   ☐ a. landlady.
   ☐ b. boss.
   ☐ c. sister.

3. One the day Hester disappeared, Pete Simpkins saw her
   ☐ a. leaving the office with Stella Dean.
   ☐ b. entering the rooming house where she lived.
   ☐ c. riding in a buggy with Stella Dean.

4. Stella was angry with Hester because
   ☐ a. their employer favored Hester.
   ☐ b. Hester was engaged to marry Stella's former fiancé.
   ☐ c. Hester made more money than she did.

5. The police
   ☐ a. could not solve the case.
   ☐ b. found that Stella had murdered Hester.
   ☐ c. suspected that Hester had merely left town.

Score 5 points for each correct answer.

_____ **Total Score:** Recalling Facts

C | Making Inferences

When you combine your own experience and information from a text to draw a conclusion that is not directly stated in that text, you are making an inference. Below are five statements that may or may not be inferences based on information in the article. Label the statements using the following key:

C—Correct Inference   F—Faulty Inference

_____ 1. Hester Holt was a very responsible person.

_____ 2. The police did not suspect Stella Dean of having any part in Hester's disappearance.

_____ 3. Stella Dean lived with her mother.

_____ 4. Hester and her sister did not get along very well.

_____ 5. Vera Cummings believed that Stella had murdered Hester.

Score 5 points for each correct answer.

_____ **Total Score:** Making Inferences

D | Using Words Precisely

Each numbered sentence below contains an underlined word or phrase from the article. Following the sentence are three definitions. One definition is closest to the meaning of the underlined word. One definition is opposite or nearly opposite. Label those two definitions using the following key. Do not label the remaining definition.

C—Closest   O—Opposite or Nearly Opposite

1. Stella returned with <u>unsettling</u> news.

   _____ a. calming

   _____ b. disturbing

   _____ c. hilarious

2. Pete Simpkins, Hester's fiancé, was as <u>mystified</u> by Hester's disappearance as Hester's sister was.

   _____ a. puzzled

   _____ b. made certain

   _____ c. thrilled

3. Although she did admit that she and Simpkins had once been engaged, Stella denied that she had any <u>animosity</u> toward Hester.

   _____ a. goodwill

   _____ b. relationship

   _____ c. hostility

4. Mrs. Bell had overheard the conversation, and her interest was <u>aroused</u>.

   _____ a. improper

   _____ b. stirred

   _____ c. deadened

5. <u>Perplexed</u>, Vera was trying to decide what to do when the door suddenly swung open by itself.

_____ a. angry

_____ b. puzzled

_____ c. with a clear and certain mind

_____ Score 3 points for each correct C answer.

_____ Score 2 points for each correct O answer.

_____ **Total Score:** Using Words Precisely

Enter the four total scores in the spaces below, and add them together to find your Reading Comprehension Score. Then record your score on the graph on page 73.

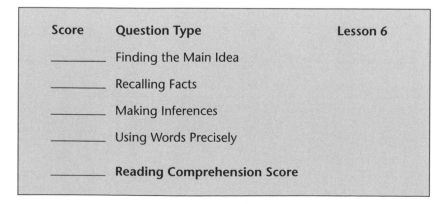

Score	Question Type	Lesson 6
_____	Finding the Main Idea	
_____	Recalling Facts	
_____	Making Inferences	
_____	Using Words Precisely	
_____	**Reading Comprehension Score**	

Author's Approach

Put an X in the box next to the correct answer.

1. The main purpose of the first paragraph is to

☐ a. describe Hester Holt.

☐ b. compare Hester Holt to Stella Dean.

☐ c. inform the reader about Denver in the early 1900s.

2. What is the author's purpose in writing "The Case of the Missing Secretary"?

☐ a. To inform the reader about Hester Holt's supposed haunting of Stella Dean

☐ b. To convey a mood of absolute terror

☐ c. To emphasize the similarities between Hester Holt and Vera Cummings

3. From the statement "Only Vera knew that Stella had died of fright," you can conclude that the author wants the reader to think that

☐ a. Vera was the only other person who had seen Hester's ghost.

☐ b. Vera had scared Stella to death.

☐ c. Vera was the only person who knew that Stella died because she had been frightened by Hester's ghost.

4. What does the author imply by saying at the end of the article "There was no mistaking the tall, slender figure of Hester Holt"?

☐ a. Hester had finally returned.

☐ b. Hester continued to haunt Stella even after Stella died.

☐ c. Hester was taller than the other secretaries in the office.

_____ Number of correct answers

Record your personal assessment of your work on the Critical Thinking Chart on page 74.

CRITICAL THINKING

Summarizing and Paraphrasing

Follow the directions provided for question 1. Put an X in the box next to the correct answer for question 2.

1. Look for the important ideas and events in paragraphs 26 and 27. Summarize those paragraphs in one or two sentences.

_____

_____

_____

2. Choose the best one-sentence paraphrase for the following sentence from the article:

   "Another witness confused the issue by stating that she had seen Hester Holt entering Mrs. Britton's rooming house on the night in question."

   ☐ a. Another witness was confused after seeing Hester question Mrs. Britton.

   ☐ b. Another witness further complicated the investigation when she said that she had seen Hester going into Mrs. Britton's rooming house that night.

   ☐ c. Another witness followed Hester into Mrs. Britton's rooming house the night Hester disappeared.

   _____ Number of correct answers

   Record your personal assessment of your work on the Critical Thinking Chart on page 74.

Critical Thinking

Follow the directions provided for questions 1, 3, and 4. Put an X in the box next to the correct answer for questions 2 and 5.

1. For each statement below, write O if it expresses an opinion and write F if it expresses a fact.

   _____ a. Stella Dean died in the office building where she had worked.

   _____ b. Stella had been engaged to Pete Simpkins.

   _____ c. Stella got what she deserved when she was tormented and frightened to death by Hester's ghost.

2. Judging from the actions of Hester's ghost as described in this article, you can predict that she will

   ☐ a. continue to follow and torment Stella.

   ☐ b. return to work and take over Stella's duties.

   ☐ c. marry Pete Simpkins.

3. Using what is told about Hester Holt and Stella Dean in the article, name three ways Hester is similar to and three ways she is different from Stella. Cite the paragraph number(s) where you found details in the article to support your conclusions.

   Similarities

   _____

   _____

   _____

CRITICAL THINKING

Differences

_____

_____

_____

4. Read paragraph 10. Then choose from the letters below to correctly complete the following statement. Write the letters on the lines.

   According to paragraph 10, _____ because _____.

   a.   Pete Simpkins broke off his engagement to Stella

   b.   Stella was furious when Pete began seeing Hester

   c.   Stella had an uncontrollable temper

5. How is the case of Hester Holt an example of a ghost story?

   ☐ a.   Her body was never found.

   ☐ b.   Stella Dean died shortly after Hester disappeared.

   ☐ c.   Witnesses claimed that they saw and heard mysterious sights and sounds at Hester's workplace shortly after her disappearance.

   _____ Number of correct answers

   Record your personal assessment of your work on the Critical Thinking Chart on page 74.

Personal Response

What was most surprising or interesting to you about this article?

_____

_____

_____

_____

Self-Assessment

The part I found most difficult about the article was

_____

_____

_____

I found this difficult because

_____

_____

_____

CRITICAL THINKING

PETER AND JENNY RUGG
Ghostly Riders in the Rain

Refreshments at the Inn *by John F. Pasmore.*
This painting shows the kind of carriage in
which Peter and Jenny Rugg could have been
riding when they were lost in the storm.

Everyone agreed that Peter Rugg was a fine man—until he got angry. When his temper flared, he could be reckless and violent. Most of the time, though, Rugg was pleasant and reasonable. A cattle dealer, he had a reputation for honesty. Some even called him generous. And whatever his flaws were, he certainly did not deserve to vanish without a trace.

2   In 1770, Rugg was living in a big house on Middle Street in Boston. His wife and his 10-year-old daughter, Jenny, lived with him. One day that fall, Rugg had to make a business trip to Concord, 20 miles outside Boston. It was a beautiful day, bright and sunny, and so Rugg invited little Jenny to come along. He knew she loved riding in the open horse-drawn carriage. She loved the way the wind blew through her hair and the sun shone on her shoulders. Besides, on flat open stretches, her father sometimes let her take the reins. Jenny always found that especially thrilling.

3   Rugg and his daughter made it to Concord without any trouble. Rugg finished his dealings there and then

headed home with Jenny. On the trip back to Boston, however, a storm erupted. The sky darkened, rain poured down in sheets, and the wind blew fiercely. In the open carriage, Jenny clung to her father's arm while he struggled to see the path through the wild storm.

4 At last, the pair made it to West Cambridge, just a few miles from home. Rugg pulled the carriage to a stop in front of Tom Cutter's house. Cutter was a friend; Rugg planned to let Jenny warm up in front of his fire and then continue his trip. Cutter welcomed Peter and Jenny into his house. He even fixed Rugg a mug of hot spiced rum. Then Cutter repeatedly insisted that Rugg spend the night.

5 "Don't be a fool, Rugg," Cutter said. "Night will soon be here, and this pelting rain could be the death of your daughter. Can you not see that the storm is increasing?"

6 Suddenly, Rugg showed a flash of his famous temper. "Let the storm increase!" he shouted at Cutter. "I will see home tonight in spite of storm or the Devil—or may I never see home!"

7 Angrily, Rugg loaded his wet and shivering daughter back into the carriage. Cutter, still hoping to dissuade him from going on, tried to grab Rugg's arm. But Rugg swung his fist out and punched

Cutter in the nose. Then, with Jenny hunched miserably beside him, Rugg set off in the carriage.

8 That was the last time anyone ever saw Peter and Jenny Rugg. Or at least it was the last time anyone ever saw them alive. They didn't made it back to Middle Street that night. Authorities searched for them for many weeks. Their bodies were never found. No sign of the carriage was ever discovered, either. At last, searchers told poor Mrs. Rugg that it was hopeless. Her husband and daughter had simply disappeared.

9 The following spring, a strange incident occurred. Late one rainy night, Thomas Felt heard a carriage clattering down Middle Street. Surprised that anyone would be out on such a foul night, Felt looked out his window. To his amazement, he saw Peter and Jenny Rugg in a rain-drenched carriage. Both father and daughter seemed to glow with an unearthly light.

10 The next morning, Felt learned that several other neighbors had heard and seen the same thing. Could it be that the ghosts of Peter and Jenny Rugg were still traveling the roads of New England?

11 As the years passed, additional sightings were reported. One witness was traveling to Boston when he was stopped

by a man in an open carriage. Seated next to the man was a little girl. Although the day was clear, both the man and the girl were soaking wet. The man asked for directions to Boston and then took off at a furious pace. As the open carriage disappeared, a storm came from nowhere and drenched everything in sight.

12 The man who collected tolls at the Charleston Bridge also saw the Ruggs. In

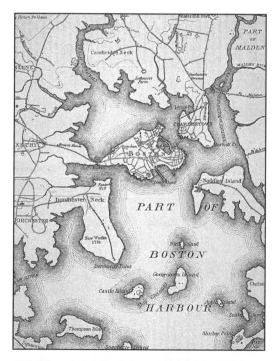

This map shows Boston and vicinity in 1776, about the time the Ruggs lived on Middle Street.

fact, he said he saw them several times. They always appeared during a rainstorm. They would come racing out of the night in their carriage and charge over the bridge without stopping to pay the toll. One night the toll collector threw a stool at them in exasperation. He was shocked when the stool passed right through the horse and hit the railing on the other side of the bridge.

13 Thirty years after Rugg and his daughter disappeared, people across New England were still seeing the ghostly carriage. Adonariah Adams saw it. He was a deliveryman who claimed to have seen the carriage one night during a thunderstorm. According to Adams, both Rugg and little Jenny were "glowing with fire like a horseshoe as it is taken from the blacksmith's hearth."

14 William Austin also saw the Ruggs. He was a passenger in a horse-drawn coach out of Boston in 1826 when the horses became nervous. Just then, an open carriage appeared on the horizon. In the carriage sat a man and a young girl. As the carriage approached Austin's coach, a wild storm blew up. Later, the driver of the coach told Austin that he often saw the weather-beaten carriage. Sometimes its owner stopped and asked directions to

Boston. But it was the oddest thing, said the stagecoach driver. The man never seemed to pay attention to the directions. He always just took off at top speed in the same direction he had been going before.

15 Despite all the sightings, no one had any hard evidence that the Ruggs ghosts were riding around New England. But that changed in the late 1820s. A minister named Samuel Nickles was traveling through Rhode Island. He rode on a good-natured old horse named Romeo. One night, Nickles and Romeo were caught in a bad storm. They were on a narrow trail between two hills when rain began pouring from the clouds. As Romeo carefully picked his way along the trail, Nickles heard a carriage approaching. It was going at a terrific speed. Looking up, he saw a man and girl riding in the carriage. Both were dripping wet. Both looked badly frightened.

16 As the carriage careened toward Nickles and his horse, Romeo reared in terror. Nickles was thrown through the air, landing on the horse that was pulling the carriage. As he clung to it for dear life, there was a huge roar of thunder and a tremendous streak of lightning. The last thing Nickles remembered was the horse and carriage bolting up the rocky ledge at

the edge of the trail. Then everything went blank.

17 Nickles awoke the next morning to find the sun shining. Romeo was grazing peacefully nearby. Thinking it had all been a dream, Nickles looked around. That's when he saw the hoof prints. They were clearly visible, burned into the hard rocky surface of the ledge. Although no one ever saw the ghosts of the two Ruggs again, the hoof prints remained there for years. The solid rock in which they were embedded was known as "Devil's Foot Rock."

If you have been timed while reading this article, enter your reading time below. Then turn to the Words-per-Minute Table on page 71 and look up your reading speed (words per minute). Enter your reading speed on the graph on page 72.

Reading Time: Lesson 7

_____ : _____
Minutes   Seconds

Finding the Main Idea

One statement below expresses the main idea of the article. One statement is too general, or too broad. The other statement explains only part of the article; it is too narrow. Label the statements using the following key:

M—Main Idea   **B—Too Broad**   **N—Too Narrow**

_____ 1. After Peter and Jenny Rugg disappeared during a rainstorm, their ghosts riding in a ghostly carriage were repeatedly seen traveling through New England.

_____ 2. The toll collector on Charleston Bridge threw a stool at the Ruggs' carriage after they crossed the bridge without paying.

_____ 3. The story of Peter and Jenny Rugg is a favorite tale in New England.

> _____ Score 15 points for a correct M answer.
>
> _____ Score 5 points for each correct B or N answer.
>
> _____ **Total Score:** Finding the Main Idea

 Recalling Facts

How well do you remember the facts in the article? Put an X in the box next to the answer that correctly completes each statement about the article.

1. Peter Rugg took his daughter Jenny with him on a business trip to
   - ☐ a. Boston.
   - ☐ b. West Cambridge.
   - ☐ c. Concord.

2. Peter Rugg stopped at Tom Cutter's house to
   - ☐ a. let Jenny warm up.
   - ☐ b. spend the night.
   - ☐ c. have a mug of hot spiced rum.

3. When Thomas Felt of Middle Street saw Peter and Jenny Rugg in a rain-drenched carriage,
   - ☐ a. the pair seemed to glow with an unearthly light.
   - ☐ b. he threw a stool at them.
   - ☐ c. Peter asked for directions to Boston.

4. Samuel Nickles was thrown from his horse Romeo when
   - ☐ a. Romeo reared in terror.
   - ☐ b. lightning and thunder struck nearby.
   - ☐ c. Romeo bolted up a rocky ledge.

5. When Nickles awoke the next morning,
   - ☐ a. he realized that it had all been a dream.
   - ☐ b. Romeo was nowhere to be seen.
   - ☐ c. he saw hoof prints burned into the ledge.

> Score 5 points for each correct answer.
>
> _____ **Total Score:** Recalling Facts

C | Making Inferences

When you combine your own experience and information from a text to draw a conclusion that is not directly stated in that text, you are making an inference. Below are five statements that may or may not be inferences based on information in the article. Label the statements using the following key:

C—Correct Inference   F—Faulty Inference

_____ 1. Peter Rugg's temper had probably gotten him into trouble before.

_____ 2. Peter Rugg would have spent the night at Cutter's house if Jenny had wanted him to stay, too.

_____ 3. Peter and Jenny Rugg died in the rainstorm.

_____ 4. Peter Rugg did not care whether Jenny wanted to stay at Tom Cutter's warm house.

_____ 5. The hoof prints burned into the rocky ledge were made by Samuel Nickles's horse Romeo.

Score 5 points for each correct answer.

_____ **Total Score:** Making Inferences

D | Using Words Precisely

Each numbered sentence below contains an underlined word or phrase from the article. Following the sentence are three definitions. One definition is closest to the meaning of the underlined word. One definition is opposite or nearly opposite. Label those two definitions using the following key. Do not label the remaining definition.

C—Closest   O—Opposite or Nearly Opposite

1. Then Cutter <u>repeatedly</u> insisted that Rugg spend the night.

_____ a. loudly

_____ b. once

_____ c. over and over again

2. Cutter, still hoping to <u>dissuade him from</u> going on, tried to grab Rugg's arm.

_____ a. convince him to

_____ b. talk him out of

_____ c. reason with him about

3. Then, with Jenny <u>hunched</u> miserably beside him, he set off in the carriage.

_____ a. sitting up straight

_____ b. wailing

_____ c. huddled

4. As the open carriage disappeared, a storm came from nowhere and <u>drenched</u> everything in sight.

_____ a. soaked

_____ b. dried out

_____ c. destroyed

5. One night the toll collector threw a stool at them in <u>exasperation</u>.

_____ a. defense

_____ b. irritation

_____ c. peacefulness

_____ Score 3 points for each correct C answer.

_____ Score 2 points for each correct O answer.

_____ **Total Score:** Using Words Precisely

Enter the four total scores in the spaces below, and add them together to find your Reading Comprehension Score. Then record your score on the graph on page 73.

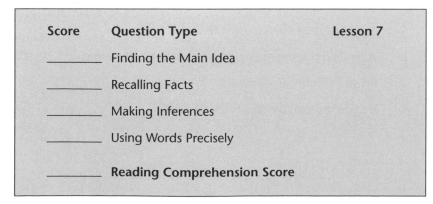

Score	Question Type	Lesson 7
_____	Finding the Main Idea	
_____	Recalling Facts	
_____	Making Inferences	
_____	Using Words Precisely	
_____	**Reading Comprehension Score**	

Author's Approach

Put an X in the box next to the correct answer.

1. What does the author mean by the statement "Suddenly, Rugg showed a flash of his famous temper"?

☐ a. Peter Rugg became angry.

☐ b. Peter Rugg felt warm and took off his coat.

☐ c. Peter Rugg was well known in New England.

2. Which of the following statements from the article best describes Peter Rugg's personality?

☐ a. "Everyone agreed that Peter Rugg was a great guy—until he got angry."

☐ b. "In 1770, Rugg was living in a big house on Middle Street in Boston."

☐ c. "His wife and his 10-year-old daughter, Jenny, lived with him."

3. What does the author imply by saying "One night the toll collector threw a stool at them in exasperation"?

☐ a. The toll collector wanted to kill Peter and Jenny Rugg.

☐ b. The toll collector was frightened of the ghostly carriage.

☐ c. The toll collector was angry because Peter Rugg never paid the toll.

4. The author probably wrote this article in order to

☐ a. encourage the reader to control his or her temper.

☐ b. describe the weather in New England.

☐ c. tell the reader about the mystery surrounding Peter and Jenny Rugg.

_____ Number of correct answers

Record your personal assessment of your work on the Critical Thinking Chart on page 74.

CRITICAL THINKING

Summarizing and Paraphrasing

Follow the directions provided for question 1. Put an X in the box next to the correct answer for question 2.

1. Complete the following one-sentence summary of the article using the lettered phrases from the phrase bank below. Write the letters on the lines.

> **Phrase Bank:**
> a. their trip to Concord
> b. the mysterious stories surrounding them after their disappearance
> c. Samuel Nickles's final sighting of the pair

After a short introduction, the article about Peter and Jenny Rugg discusses _____, goes on to explain _____, and ends with _____.

2. Choose the sentence that correctly restates the following sentence from the article:

"Nickles was thrown through the air, landing on the horse that was pulling the carriage."

☐ a. Nickles was thrown off the horse that was pulling the Ruggs' carriage.

☐ b. After Nickles was thrown from his horse, he landed on the one pulling the Ruggs' carriage.

☐ c. Nickles flew through the air and landed on his own horse.

_____ Number of correct answers

Record your personal assessment of your work on the Critical Thinking Chart on page 74.

Critical Thinking

Put an X in the box next to the correct answer for questions 1, 4, and 5. Follow the directions provided for the other questions.

1. From the article, you can predict that if Peter Rugg had agreed to spend the night at Tom Cutter's house,

☐ a. Jenny would have died in his home.

☐ b. Peter and Jenny would not have disappeared that night.

☐ c. Peter would have murdered his friend.

2. Choose from the letters below to correctly complete the following statement. Write the letters on the lines.

In the article, _____ and _____ gave similar descriptions of the glow that surrounded the people in the ghostly carriage.

a. Adonariah Adams

b. Thomas Felt

c. Samuel Nickles

3. Think about cause-effect relationships in the article. Fill in the blanks in the cause-effect chart, drawing from the letters below.

Cause	Effect
_____	Peter invited Jenny to go to Concord.
_____	Peter punched him in the nose.
The Ruggs' carriage sped toward Nickles.	_____

a. Tom Cutter pestered Rugg about spending the night.

b. It was a bright, sunny day.

c. He was thrown from his rearing horse.

4. Of the following theme categories, which would this story fit into?

☐ a.   Never travel in a rainstorm.

☐ b.   Never ride a horse on a narrow trail.

☐ c.   Never let your emotions get the better of you.

5. What did you have to do to answer question 2?

☐ a.   find a cause (why something happened)

☐ b.   draw a conclusion (a sensible statement based on the text and your experience)

☐ c.   find a comparison (how things are alike)

_____ Number of correct answers

Record your personal assessment of your work on the Critical Thinking Chart on page 74.

Personal Response

Would you recommend this article to other students? Explain.

_____

_____

_____

Self-Assessment

One of the things I did best when reading this article was

_____

_____

_____

_____

I believe I did this well because

_____

_____

_____

_____

Compare and Contrast

Think about the articles you have read in Unit One. Pick the four apparitions you think are easiest to believe in. Write the titles of the articles that tell about them in the first column of the chart below. Use information you learned from the articles to fill in the empty boxes in the chart.

Title	What evidence do you find most convincing?	Which evidence raises doubts about the truthfulness or accuracy of the witnesses' accounts?	What explanations, besides the existence of ghosts, can you suggest for the occurrences in this article?

If I could choose any apparition to investigate, it would be _____. I would follow this procedure to find the truth: _____

_____

_____

Words-per-Minute Table

Unit One

Directions: If you were timed while reading an article, refer to the Reading Time you recorded in the box at the end of the article. Use this words-per-minute table to determine your reading speed for that article. Then plot your reading speed on the graph on page 72.

Lesson No. of Words	Sample 885	1 1550	2 934	3 977	4 1284	5 1450	6 1480	7 1198	
1:30	590	1033	623	651	856	967	987	799	90
1:40	531	930	560	586	770	870	888	719	100
1:50	483	845	509	533	700	791	807	653	110
2:00	443	775	467	489	642	725	740	599	120
2:10	408	715	431	451	593	669	683	553	130
2:20	379	664	400	419	550	621	634	513	140
2:30	354	620	374	391	514	580	592	479	150
2:40	332	581	350	366	482	544	555	449	160
2:50	312	547	330	345	453	512	522	423	170
3:00	295	517	311	326	428	483	493	399	180
3:10	279	489	295	309	405	458	467	378	190
3:20	266	465	280	293	385	435	444	359	200
3:30	253	443	267	279	367	414	423	342	210
3:40	241	423	255	266	350	395	404	327	220
3:50	231	404	244	255	335	378	386	313	230
4:00	221	388	234	244	321	363	370	300	240
4:10	212	372	224	234	308	348	355	288	250
4:20	204	358	216	225	296	335	342	276	260
4:30	197	344	208	217	285	322	329	266	270
4:40	190	332	200	209	275	311	317	257	280
4:50	183	321	193	202	266	300	306	248	290
5:00	177	310	187	195	257	290	296	240	300
5:10	171	300	181	189	249	281	286	232	310
5:20	166	291	175	183	241	272	278	225	320
5:30	161	282	170	178	233	264	269	218	330
5:40	156	274	165	172	227	256	261	211	340
5:50	152	266	160	167	220	249	254	205	350
6:00	148	258	156	163	214	242	247	200	360
6:10	144	251	151	158	208	235	240	194	370
6:20	140	245	147	154	203	229	234	189	380
6:30	136	238	144	150	198	223	228	184	390
6:40	133	233	140	147	193	218	222	180	400
6:50	130	227	137	143	188	212	217	175	410
7:00	126	221	133	140	183	207	211	171	420
7:10	123	216	130	136	179	202	207	167	430
7:20	121	211	127	133	175	198	202	163	440
7:30	118	207	125	130	171	193	197	160	450
7:40	115	202	122	127	167	189	193	156	460
7:50	113	198	119	125	164	185	189	153	470
8:00	111	194	117	122	161	181	185	150	480

Minutes and Seconds / Seconds

Plotting Your Progress: Reading Speed

Unit One

Directions: If you were timed while reading an article, write your words-per-minute rate for that article in the box under the number of the lesson. Then plot your reading speed on the graph by putting a small X on the line directly above the number of the lesson, across from the number of words per minute you read. As you mark your speed for each lesson, graph your progress by drawing a line to connect the X's.

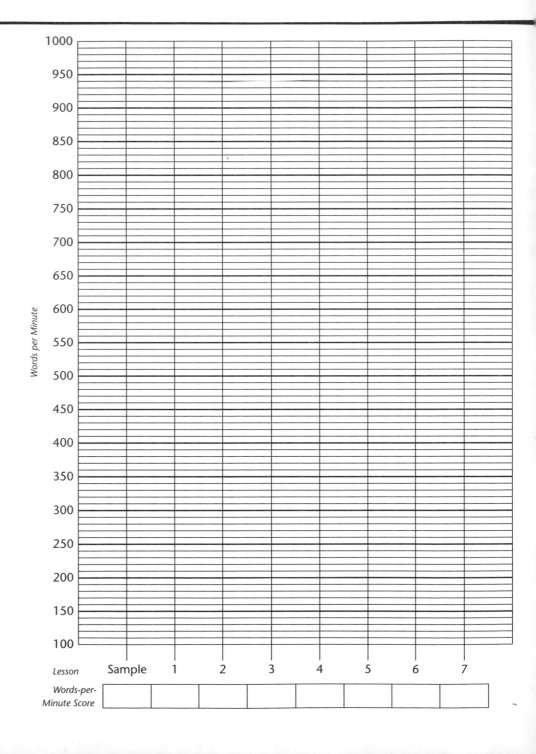

Lesson	Sample	1	2	3	4	5	6	7
Words-per-Minute Score								

Plotting Your Progress: Reading Comprehension

Unit One

Directions: Write your Reading Comprehension score for each lesson in the box under the number of the lesson. Then plot your score on the graph by putting a small X on the line directly above the number of the lesson and across from the score you earned. As you mark your score for each lesson, graph your progress by drawing a line to connect the X's.

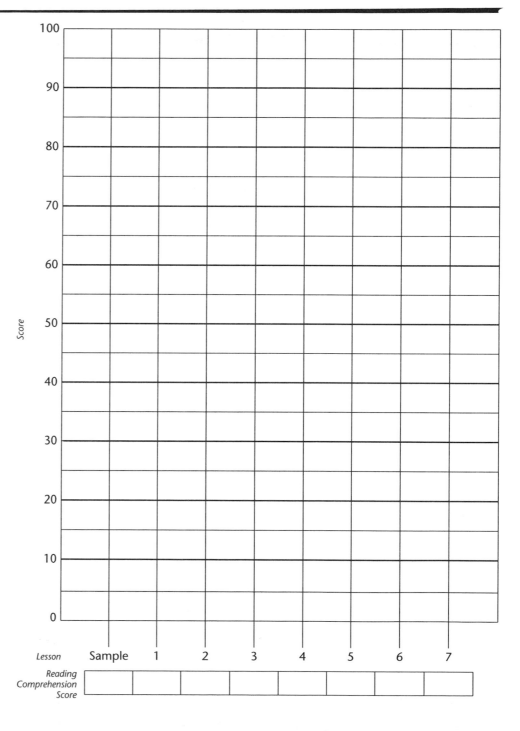

Lesson	Sample	1	2	3	4	5	6	7
Reading Comprehension Score								

Plotting Your Progress: Critical Thinking

Unit One

Directions: Work with your teacher to evaluate your responses to the Critical Thinking questions for each lesson. Then fill in the appropriate spaces in the chart below. For each lesson and each type of Critical Thinking question, do the following: Mark a minus sign (–) in the box to indicate areas in which you feel you could improve. Mark a plus sign (+) to indicate areas in which you feel you did well. Mark a minus-slash-plus sign (–/+) to indicate areas in which you had mixed success. Then write any comments you have about your performance, including ideas for improvement.

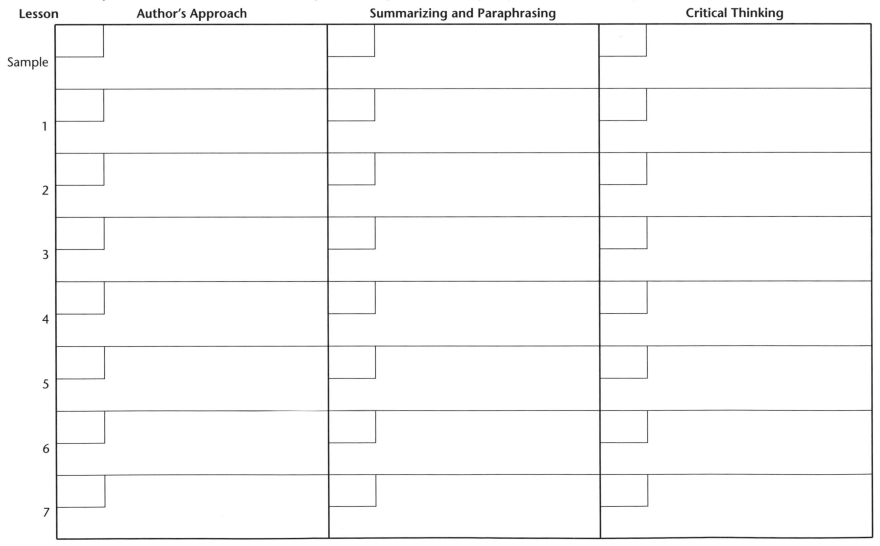

Lesson	Author's Approach	Summarizing and Paraphrasing	Critical Thinking
Sample			
1			
2			
3			
4			
5			
6			
7			

UNIT TWO

OSCEOLA'S HEAD

Seminole chief Osceola (pictured here) was lured into a trap by a U.S. general and imprisoned in the jail at Castillo de San Marcos in 1835.

It had been another busy day at Castillo de San Marcos. Hundreds of tourists had visited the old fort in St. Augustine, Florida. They had peered into the musty dungeons. They had taken pictures of one another on the wide battlements. As the day came to a close, they solemnly watched the flag being lowered.

2   A few people lingered long after the sun had set. They glanced expectantly, and perhaps nervously, at the high walls of the fort, bathed in silvery moonlight. Would they see it? they wondered. Would they see the ghostly head of Osceola floating above the fort?

3   To understand what those people were looking for, we must go back in time to a warm October day in 1837. On that day a tall Indian man stood with his hands clasped behind his back, gazing intently into the waters of a shallow creek. He was Osceola, a proud chief of the Seminole tribe of Florida.

4   Osceola's reflection revealed a handsome man with dark eyes, high cheekbones, and a light complexion. He owed the color of his skin to his father, an

English trader. But he was very much an Indian, for his mother was a Creek. The Seminole were originally part of the Creek confederation of tribes in Alabama and Georgia. When some of them moved south into Florida, they became known as Seminole, meaning "runaways."

5 Osceola was not admiring his reflection in the water that day. He was deep in thought. It was the day the Seminole might finally get their lands back.

6 For more than 100 years, the Seminole had lived peacefully in Florida. Then white settlers had taken their lands. In 1835 the federal government attempted to force the Seminole to sign a treaty that would require them to move west to what is now Oklahoma.

7 "Why should we leave our homelands?" Osceola asked. Most of the other Seminole leaders agreed with him. They voted not to sign the treaty. Instead, they vowed to fight for their rights until the last drop of Seminole blood had been shed. Osceola was chosen to lead the struggle.

8 The fighting began, and it was terrible. The Seminole raided village after village, killing the settlers. In turn, government soldiers chased the Seminole back into the swampy forests of Florida. Many lives were lost on both sides, but it was clear that the Seminole were not about to surrender. Finally, General Thomas Jesup, the leader of the government forces, had an idea. He invited Osceola to meet with him under a flag of truce to talk peace.

9 Osceola agreed to talk, for he too was tired of the bloodshed. His body ached with weariness brought on by bouts of yellow fever that sapped his strength. He was eager to end the war.

Castillo de San Marcos is now a national monument in St. Augustine, Florida.

10   The day of the meeting arrived. Osceola, together with a handful of other Seminole leaders whom he had brought with him, waited at the appointed place. Each warrior had a square of white cloth—the flag of truce—tied to his rifle.

11   There was to be no peace talk, however. General Jesup had laid a trap, not the groundwork for peace. Two hundred soldiers rode up and seized Osceola and his companions.

12   The Seminole leaders were thrown into jail in the old fort of Castillo de San Marcos in St. Augustine. When word of General Jesup's deception got out, the whole country was outraged. Still, Jesup refused to release Osceola. He believed that without Osceola's leadership the Seminole resistance would collapse. It did not, and the war went on.

13   As 1837 drew to a close, Osceola, who had been joined by his family, was moved to a prison in Fort Moultrie, South Carolina. The fever that had long plagued him now confined him to his bed. He knew his end was near.

14   On the morning of January 30, 1838, Osceola readied himself for death. He dressed in his finest clothes. Around his head he wound a turban. Into the turban he stuck three feathers: one red, one white, and one blue. He painted half of his face and neck with red war paint. Without a word, he solemnly shook the hands of his family and friends. Then he called for his favorite scalping knife. Clasping the knife, he crossed his hands on his chest. He drew one more breath,

smiled, and died. Osceola was about 35 years old.

15   Dr. Frederick Wheedon, who had been treating Osceola at the prison, prepared the chief's body for burial. The funeral that followed drew hundreds of admirers who wanted to pay their respects to the great warrior and leader. How surprised they would have been to learn what was—or rather what was not—in the wooden coffin they saw lowered into the ground.

16   Did Osceola's death mean the end of war with the Seminole? No, indeed. In fact, the fighting continued for five more years. Finally, realizing they would never defeat the Seminole, the government simply quit fighting. To this day, the Seminole own their lands in Florida. They are the only Indian tribe ever to refuse to sign a treaty with the government.

17   Osceola was eventually returned to his home. Many years after his death, when Florida had become the 27th state, the government decided that Osceola should be reburied in the land he had fought so hard to defend.

18   When his coffin was dug up for the move, officials decided to open it and look inside. What a surprise they got! Osceola's skull was missing. It seems that Dr. Wheedon, for reasons he never disclosed, had cut off Osceola's head when he prepared the body for burial. He took the head to his home in St. Augustine. It passed through many hands over the years, finally ending up in a museum in New York City. In 1866 a fire ravaged part of the museum, and Osceola's head was destroyed.

19   Or was it? Many visitors to the old fort of Castillo de San Marcos claim to have seen the head. It is said that on moonlit nights the head often appears, hovering above the very cell in which Osceola was imprisoned. It is wrapped in a turban decorated with three feathers: one red, one white, and one blue.

20   Is it possible that Osceola's ghostly head does appear over the fort, or do active imaginations play tricks on people's eyes? If the apparition is real, why does Osceola return? Some believers think he wants to remind people of his struggles to save the Seminole lands. Others think he wants to be reunited with his remains. Perhaps he wishes to continue to inspire his people. Whether or not Osceola does visit Castillo de San Marcos, the story of Osceola's head reminds people about the struggle of the Seminole and about a brave leader. 🍃

If you have been timed while reading this article, enter your reading time below. Then turn to the Words-per-Minute Table on page 133 and look up your reading speed (words per minute). Enter your reading speed on the graph on page 134.

Reading Time: **Lesson 8**

_____ : _____
Minutes   Seconds

Finding the Main Idea

One statement below expresses the main idea of the article. One statement is too general, or too broad. The other statement explains only part of the article; it is too narrow. Label the statements using the following key:

M—Main Idea   **B—Too Broad**   **N—Too Narrow**

_____ 1. The father of Osceola, the brave leader of the Seminole, was an English trader and his mother was a Creek.

_____ 2. Occasionally, observers report seeing the head of the brave Seminole chief Osceola floating above Castillo de San Marcos where he was held prisoner during the Seminole Wars.

_____ 3. The apparition of Seminole chief Osceola attracts and inspires many people who are interested in the history of the chief.

_____ Score 15 points for a correct M answer.

_____ Score 5 points for each correct B or N answer.

_____ **Total Score:** Finding the Main Idea

 Recalling Facts

How well do you remember the facts in the article? Put an X in the box next to the answer that correctly completes each statement about the article.

1. When Osceola died he was about
   ☐ a. 35 years old.
   ☐ b. 37 years old.
   ☐ c. 25 years old.

2. Osceola's father was
   ☐ a. an English trader.
   ☐ b. a Creek Indian.
   ☐ c. a Seminole.

3. Osceola died in
   ☐ a. Florida.
   ☐ b. Georgia
   ☐ c. South Carolina.

4. The U.S. Government's war with the Seminole
   ☐ a. ended in 1837.
   ☐ b. went on for seven years.
   ☐ c. ended when Osceola was captured.

5. The Seminole
   ☐ a. never signed a treaty.
   ☐ b. eventually surrendered.
   ☐ c. lost their lands in Florida.

Score 5 points for each correct answer.

_____ **Total Score:** Recalling Facts

C | Making Inferences

When you combine your own experience and information from a text to draw a conclusion that is not directly stated in that text, you are making an inference. Below are five statements that may or may not be inferences based on information in the article. Label the statements using the following key:

C—Correct Inference   F—Faulty Inference

_____ 1. General Jesup honored the rules of war.

_____ 2. The Seminole were a stubborn people.

_____ 3. The Seminole owned desirable land in Florida.

_____ 4. The United States Government eventually recognized Osceola's contributions to Florida.

_____ 5. The Seminole loved war.

Score 5 points for each correct answer.

_____ **Total Score:** Making Inferences

D | Using Words Precisely

Each numbered sentence below contains an underlined word or phrase from the article. Following the sentence are three definitions. One definition is closest to the meaning of the underlined word. One definition is opposite or nearly opposite. Label those two definitions using the following key. Do not label the remaining definition.

C—Closest   O—Opposite or Nearly Opposite

1. On that day a tall Indian man stood with his hands clasped behind his back, gazing <u>intently</u> into the waters of a shallow creek.

    _____ a. with great anger

    _____ b. with concentration

    _____ c. without concern

2. His body ached with weariness brought on by bouts of yellow fever that <u>sapped</u> his strength.

    _____ a. exercised

    _____ b. increased

    _____ c. drained

3. When word of General Jesup's <u>deception</u> got out, the whole country was outraged.

    _____ a. reputation

    _____ b. trickery

    _____ c. honesty

4. Without a word, he <u>solemnly</u> shook the hands of his family and friends.

_____ a. cheerfully

_____ b. sadly

_____ c. politely

5. In 1866 a fire <u>ravaged</u> part of the museum, and Osceola's head was destroyed.

_____ a. restored

_____ b. destroyed

_____ c. flared up

_____ Score 3 points for each correct C answer.

_____ Score 2 points for each correct O answer.

_____ **Total Score:** Using Words Precisely

Enter the four total scores in the spaces below, and add them together to find your Reading Comprehension Score. Then record your score on the graph on page 135.

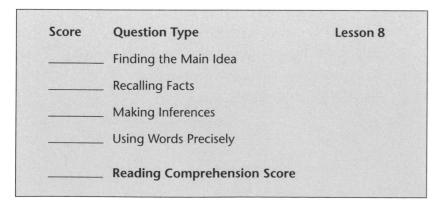

Score	Question Type	Lesson 8
_____	Finding the Main Idea	
_____	Recalling Facts	
_____	Making Inferences	
_____	Using Words Precisely	
_____	**Reading Comprehension Score**	

Author's Approach

Put an X in the box next to the correct answer.

1. What does the author mean by the statement "Instead, they vowed to fight for their rights until the last drop of Seminole blood had been shed"?

☐ a. The Seminole were bloodthirsty warriors.

☐ b. The Seminole didn't value their lives anymore.

☐ c. The Seminole were prepared to die to defend their rights.

2. What is the author's purpose in writing "Osceola's Head"?

☐ a. To express an opinion about the U.S. Government's treatment of the Seminole

☐ b. To tell the reader about Osceola's life and death

☐ c. To inform the reader about the plight of Native Americans in the 1800s

3. How is the author's purpose for writing the article expressed in paragraph 11?

☐ a. The author criticizes General Jesup for trapping Osceola.

☐ b. The author explains how Native Americans were often tricked in the 19th century.

☐ c. The author describes Osceola's capture by General Jesup.

_____ Number of correct answers

Record your personal assessment of your work on the Critical Thinking Chart on page 136.

Summarizing and Paraphrasing

Follow the directions provided for question 1. Put an X in the box next to the correct answer for the other questions.

1. Look for the important ideas and events in paragraphs 13 and 14. Summarize those paragraphs in one or two sentences.

_____

_____

_____

2. Below are summaries of the article. Choose the summary that says all the most important things about the article but in the fewest words.

☐ a. After refusing to sign a treaty with the United States, Seminole chief Osceola was captured and imprisoned. When he died shortly thereafter, the physician who treated Osceola cut off and kept his head. Today, some people say that Osceola's head often appears, floating over the fort where he had been imprisoned.

☐ b. Osceola refused to sign a treaty that would require the Seminole to leave their land. As a result, he was captured and imprisoned by U.S. Government forces. Osceola died in prison from yellow fever, wearing a turban with three feathers stuck in it. Visitors to the fort where Osceola was imprisoned claim to have seen his ghostly head and turban hovering in the air over his cell.

☐ c. The sight of Osceola's head floating over the prison where he stayed for years should remind us of the struggle of the Seminole.

3. Choose the best one-sentence paraphrase for the following sentence from the article:

"It seems that Dr. Wheedon, for reasons he never disclosed, had cut off Osceola's head when he prepared the body for burial."

☐ a. Some people believe that Dr. Wheedon cut off Osceola's head, but no one knows for sure.

☐ b. Although no one knows why, Dr. Wheedon apparently had cut off Osceola's head before the body was buried.

☐ c. Dr. Wheedon had cut off Osceola's head, but he refused to talk about it when people asked him why.

_____ Number of correct answers

Record your personal assessment of your work on the Critical Thinking Chart on page 136.

Critical Thinking

Put an X in the box next to the correct answer for questions 1, 4, and 5. Follow the directions provided for questions 2 and 3.

1. Judging from Osceola's actions as told in this article, you can predict that if he had been released, he would have

☐ a. continued to fight the government forces until he died.

☐ b. set a trap for General Jesup to pay him back.

☐ c. urged his people to sign the treaty.

2. Choose from the letters below to correctly complete the following statement. Write the letters on the lines.

On the positive side, _____, but on the negative side _____.

a. Osceola died as a prisoner of the U.S. Government forces

b. Osceola wrapped his head in a feathered turban before he died

c. the Seminole did not lose their lands in Florida

3. Choose from the letters below to correctly complete the following statement. Write the letters on the lines.

According to the article, _____ caused officials to _____, and the effect was _____.

a. open his coffin

b. they discovered his head was missing

c. Florida's decision to rebury Osceola

4. How is the story of Osceola an example of a ghost story?

☐ a. Osceola's head was cut off for unknown reasons.

☐ b. Osceola was a hero of his people.

☐ c. At times, people claim to have seen Osceola's detached head floating over the cell where he had been imprisoned.

5. What did you have to do to answer question 1?

☐ a. find a cause (why something happened)

☐ b. find a comparison (how things are the same)

☐ c. make a prediction (what might happen next)

_____ Number of correct answers

Record your personal assessment of your work on the Critical Thinking Chart on page 136.

Personal Response

How do you think General Jesup felt when Osceola died?

_____

_____

_____

_____

Self-Assessment

Before reading this article, I already knew

_____

_____

_____

_____

CRITICAL THINKING

WHALEY HOUSE

Whaley House in San Diego's Old Town was built between May 6, 1856, and May 10, 1857.

Welcome to Whaley House," said June Reading with a smile. It was October 9, 1960, and the guests were a Dr. and Mrs. Kirbey from British Columbia, Canada. June Reading was director of the historic house, which stands as one of the finest remaining examples of early American architecture.

2   Built in the Old Town section of San Diego, California, in 1857, Whaley House was restored and turned into a historical museum in 1957. It opened to the public in April 1960.

3   After signing in, the Kirbeys wandered by themselves through the gracious home that San Diego pioneer Thomas Whaley had built for his wife and six children. Downstairs are a parlor, a music room, a library, and the kitchen. A large one-story annex is attached to the first-floor rooms. Upstairs are four large bedrooms.

4   Mrs. Kirbey loved old houses. In fact, she considered herself something of an expert in early architecture. But in Whaley House she found more than she had bargained for.

5   "Have you ever noticed anything unusual about the upstairs?" Mrs. Kirbey

asked June Reading, when she had completed her wanderings. "What do you mean?" asked June Reading. "When I started upstairs," Mrs. Kirbey began, "I felt a breeze over my head. I didn't see anything, but I felt a pressure against me that made it hard to continue up the stairs. Then when I looked into the rooms, I had the feeling that someone was standing behind me. The person was so close I expected a tap on my shoulder!"

6   At the time, June Reading did not know what to make of this. True, she herself had occasionally heard odd noises, such as the sound of heavy footsteps, but she had never experienced anything like what Mrs. Kirbey had related.

7   June Reading next led the Kirbeys to the annex, which had once served as the San Diego County Courthouse. When they entered the annex, Mrs. Kirbey stopped dead in her tracks. "Someone is here," she whispered. Neither June Reading nor Dr. Kirbey saw anyone.

8   "Can you describe what it is you are seeing?" June Reading asked. "I see a small figure, that of a woman who has a swarthy complexion. She is wearing a long, full skirt that reaches to the floor. The skirt appears to be made of calico or gingham cloth, with a small print. She has a kind of cap on her head, dark eyes, and she is wearing gold hoops in her pierced ears. She seems to be staying in this room—living here, I gather. I get the impression we are sort of invading her privacy."

9   After the Kirbeys left, June Reading pondered long and hard about the incident. Mrs. Kirbey did not seem to be the kind of person who would make up such a story, but could it be that there were actually ghosts in Whaley House?

10   Baffled by the incident, June Reading tried to forget it, but she couldn't, for the sound of footsteps in the house continued. "For the next six months," she later said, "I often found myself going upstairs to see if someone was actually there." No one ever was.

11   June Reading was not the only person to hear strange noises in Whaley House. Workmen often commented on eerie sounds, and so did several volunteer guides. Eventually, still stranger things began happening.

12   Starting in October 1962, windows on the upper level of the house would suddenly and inexplicably fly open. June Reading had bolts installed to ensure that the windows would remain shut. They did, but then the burglar alarms began ringing at odd hours.

13   In the months that followed, Whaley House volunteers reported literally scores of strange occurrences. One volunteer reported hearing music and a woman's voice singing "Home Again." He said he later heard organ music, but when he investigated, he found the music room empty and the organ covered. Another volunteer reported seeing a woman dressed in a hoop skirt. A third told of coming upon "the figure of a man, clad in a frock coat and pantaloons," and a dog, "spotted…like a fox terrier, that ran with its ears flapping, down the hall and into

Psychic Sybil Leek tried to communicate with the spirits haunting Whaley House.

the dining room." Still others told of seeing a rocking chair moving for no apparent reason, and of smelling cigar smoke and perfume.

14   These incidents might well have gone unrecorded had it not been for a local TV personality, Regis Philbin. Believing that the strange goings-on at Whaley House would make an interesting subject for his show, Philbin set up a program that featured the well-known ghost hunter Hans Holzer, June Reading, a medium, and himself.

15   On June 25, 1965, Philbin, Holzer, a TV crew, and the medium, an English woman named Sybil Leek, met June Reading at Whaley House. Sybil Leek had been told nothing of the strange occurrences, yet from the first, she felt "presences" in the house. She immediately felt drawn to the kitchen. As she was on the way to that room, an apparition presented itself. "A child came down the stairs and I followed her," said Sybil.

16   Later, on live TV, Sybil Leek appeared to withdraw into a trance. Many mediums try to communicate with spirits by entering into trances. While Sybil was in the trance, a voice quite unlike her own emanated from her lips. It spoke of four ghosts in Whaley House. One was that of a man who often wore heavy boots, opened windows, and rang bells—Thomas Whaley himself. A second was that of Annabelle, a friend of the Whaleys, who had died at the age of 13, of poisoning from some food she had taken from the

Whaley House kitchen. The strange voice went on to say that the organ music came from Anna Lannay, Thomas Whaley's wife, who had died in the house in 1913. And who was the fourth ghost? It was that of a man called Yankee Jim Robinson. Unjustly charged with stealing a boat, Yankee Jim was hanged in 1852 on the very site where Whaley House would be built five years later.

17   So the ghosts of Whaley House now had identities. But *why* were they haunting the house? Well, it's often said in ghost stories that the spirits of people return because they are uneasy, because they have suffered some great injustice, or because they have left something unsettled. Do any of those reasons fit the four ghosts?

18   Thomas Whaley suffered an injustice. In 1869 he signed a contract with the county of San Diego, agreeing to build an annex onto his house to be leased by the county as a courthouse. He built the annex, but after two years the county broke its lease. Whaley, understandably furious about the breach of contract, petitioned to be reimbursed for building the annex. The matter was never settled. Mrs. Whaley, it can be presumed, also suffered in this matter.

19   Yankee Jim suffered an even more profound injustice. He was hanged for a crime he did not commit.

20   As for the youngster Annabelle, maybe she just liked the Whaleys so much that she didn't want to part from them. During

her short life, she spent more time at their house than she did in her own.

21   Whatever the reasons, the ghostly signs continue in Whaley House. In fact, Whaley House is regarded as one of the most actively haunted houses in the world. People claim that Thomas Whaley roams his house, the odor of his beloved Havana cigars trailing behind him. Organ music and singing are heard, and the fragrance of Mrs. Whaley's violet-scented perfume wafts unaccountably through the air. The apparition of a young girl continues to materialize in the kitchen. And Yankee Jim still reportedly wanders the grounds.

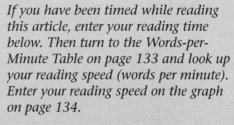

If you have been timed while reading this article, enter your reading time below. Then turn to the Words-per-Minute Table on page 133 and look up your reading speed (words per minute). Enter your reading speed on the graph on page 134.

Reading Time: Lesson 9

_____ : _____
Minutes   Seconds

A Finding the Main Idea

One statement below expresses the main idea of the article. One statement is too general, or too broad. The other statement explains only part of the article; it is too narrow. Label the statements using the following key:

M—Main Idea   B—Too Broad   N—Too Narrow

_____ 1. Many people have reportedly witnessed strange and unexplainable occurrences in Whaley House in California.

_____ 2. A medium named Sybil Leek claimed to have made contact with a spirit who told of ghosts living in Whaley House.

_____ 3. Whaley House, a historic house in California, is supposedly actively haunted by four ghosts.

_____ Score 15 points for a correct M answer.

_____ Score 5 points for each correct B or N answer.

_____ **Total Score:** Finding the Main Idea

B Recalling Facts

How well do you remember the facts in the article? Put an X in the box next to the answer that correctly completes each statement about the article.

1. The first signs that ghosts occupied Whaley House occurred
   ☐ a. shortly after the last owners died.
   ☐ b. just before the house opened as a museum.
   ☐ c. soon after the house was opened to the public.

2. Thomas Whaley built an addition onto his house to be used as
   ☐ a. a courthouse.
   ☐ b. bedrooms for his growing family.
   ☐ c. an office.

3. In 1969 Whaley House was featured on a TV
   ☐ a. news program.
   ☐ b. variety show.
   ☐ c. talk show.

4. The young girl whose ghost materializes in Whaley House was
   ☐ a. a friend of the family.
   ☐ b. a servant in the house.
   ☐ c. the Whaleys' niece.

5. Mrs. Kirbey was
   ☐ a. the acting director of Whaley House.
   ☐ b. a visitor to Whaley House.
   ☐ c. a medium.

Score 5 points for each correct answer.

_____ **Total Score:** Recalling Facts

C | Making Inferences

When you combine your own experience and information from a text to draw a conclusion that is not directly stated in that text, you are making an inference. Below are five statements that may or may not be inferences based on information in the article. Label the statements using the following key:

C—Correct Inference   **F—Faulty Inference**

_____ 1. Whaley House had become run down before people decided to turn it into a museum.

_____ 2. Mrs. Kirbey believed in ghosts.

_____ 3. Thomas Whaley was a well-known and respected man in San Diego.

_____ 4. Sybil Leek was a fraud.

_____ 5. Annabelle had probably been purposely poisoned by someone in the Whaley house.

Score 5 points for each correct answer.

_____ **Total Score:** Making Inferences

D | Using Words Precisely

Each numbered sentence below contains an underlined word or phrase from the article. Following the sentence are three definitions. One definition is closest to the meaning of the underlined word. One definition is opposite or nearly opposite. Label those two definitions using the following key. Do not label the remaining definition.

C—Closest   **O—Opposite or Nearly Opposite**

1. True, she herself had occasionally heard odd noises, such as the sound of heavy footsteps, but she had never experienced anything like what Mrs. Kirbey had <u>related</u>.

_____ a. told about

_____ b. kept secret

_____ c. done

2. After the Kirbeys left, June Reading <u>pondered</u> long and hard about the incident.

_____ a. thought

_____ b. ignored

_____ c. laughed

3. While Sybil was in the trance, a voice quite unlike her own <u>emanated</u> from her lips.

_____ a. came forth

_____ b. whistled

_____ c. became trapped

4. Whaley, understandably furious about the breach of contract, <u>petitioned</u> to be reimbursed for building the annex.

_____ a. demanded

_____ b. requested

_____ c. voted

5. Yankee Jim suffered an even more <u>profound</u> injustice.

_____ a. minor

_____ b. great

_____ c. absurd

_____ Score 3 points for each correct C answer.

_____ Score 2 points for each correct O answer.

_____ **Total Score:** Using Words Precisely

Enter the four total scores in the spaces below, and add them together to find your Reading Comprehension Score. Then record your score on the graph on page 135.

Score	Question Type	Lesson 9
_____	Finding the Main Idea	
_____	Recalling Facts	
_____	Making Inferences	
_____	Using Words Precisely	
_____	**Reading Comprehension Score**	

Author's Approach

Put an X in the box next to the correct answer.

1. From the statements below, choose those that you believe the author would agree with.

   ☐ a. Mrs. Kirbey made up her story about seeing a ghost in Whaley House.

   ☐ b. Regis Philbin's television show helped make the hauntings at Whaley House famous.

   ☐ c. Yankee Jim Robinson should not have been hanged as a thief.

2. From the statement "Mrs. Kirbey did not seem to be the kind of person who would make up such a story," you can conclude that the author wants the reader to think that Mrs. Kirbey

   ☐ a. had no imagination.

   ☐ b. was a nut.

   ☐ c. could be trusted.

3. In this article, "But in Whaley House [Mrs. Kirbey] found more than she had bargained for" means

   ☐ a. the house cost less than Mrs. Kirbey thought.

   ☐ b. there were more features to the house than Mrs. Kirbey could have expected.

   ☐ c. Mrs. Kirbey found more bargains in the house than she had thought possible.

4. Choose the statement below that best describes the author's position in paragraph 21.

☐ a. Many people believe that Whaley House really is haunted.

☐ b. Whaley House has been proved to be one of the most haunted houses in the world.

☐ c. The author cannot understand why anyone believes that Whaley House is haunted.

_____ Number of correct answers

Record your personal assessment of your work on the Critical Thinking Chart on page 136.

Summarizing and Paraphrasing

Follow the directions provided for questions 1 and 2. Put an X in the box next to the correct answer for question 3.

1. Complete the following one-sentence summary of the article using the lettered phrases from the phrase bank below. Write the letters on the lines.

Phrase Bank:
a. Sybil Leek's identification of the ghosts
b. Mrs. Kirbey's visit and ghost sighting
c. other strange sights, sounds, and happenings in the house

The article about Whaley House begins with _____, goes on to explain _____, and ends with _____.

2. Reread paragraph 16 in the article. Below, write a summary of the paragraph in no more than 25 words.

_____

_____

_____

_____

Reread your summary and decide whether it covers the important ideas in the paragraph. Next, try to shorten the summary to about 15 words or less without leaving out any essential information. Write this summary below.

_____

_____

3. Choose the sentence that correctly restates the following sentence from the article:

"Baffled by the incident, June Reading tried to forget it, but she couldn't, for the sound of footsteps in the house continued."

☐ a. June Reading tried to forget about the footsteps, but she couldn't because she was so confused.

☐ b. June Reading tried to forget about the puzzling incident, but the sound of footsteps in the house kept reminding her of it.

☐ c. June Reading was confused by the sound of footsteps in the house.

_____ Number of correct answers

Record your personal assessment of your work on the Critical Thinking Chart on page 136.

CRITICAL THINKING

Critical Thinking

Follow the directions provided for question 1. Put an X in the box next to the correct answer for the other questions.

1. For each statement below, write O if it expresses an opinion and write F if it expresses a fact.

_____ a. Everyone agrees that Whaley House is the most haunted house in the world.

_____ b. Whaley House was opened to the public as a historical museum in 1960.

_____ c. Regis Philbin featured the Whaley House and its hauntings on his television program.

2. Judging by events in the article, you can predict that the following will happen next:

☐ a. People will continue to report seeing apparitions in the Whaley House.

☐ b. The Whaley House will be torn down in an effort to rid it of its ghosts.

☐ c. Tourists, fearful of the Whaley House's reputation, will no longer visit the historic house.

3. What was the effect of Regis Philbin's decision to invite Sybil Leek on his television program?

☐ a. The strange incidents at Whaley House went unrecorded.

☐ b. The medium communicated with the spirits in Whaley House.

☐ c. Philbin thought Whaley House would make an interesting subject.

4. What did you have to do to answer question 3?

☐ a. find a definition (what something means)

☐ b. find an effect (something that happened)

☐ c. find a comparison (how things are the same)

_____ Number of correct answers

Record your personal assessment of your work on the Critical Thinking Chart on page 136.

Personal Response

Describe a time when you heard strange sounds at night.

_____

_____

_____

_____

Self-Assessment

While reading the article, I found it easiest to

_____

_____

_____

_____

ROLAND'S EXORCISM

The 1974 film The Exorcist *was based on the story of Roland's exorcism. In this scene from the film, a priest arrives at the possessed girl's home to begin the exorcism ritual.*

Even today, no one knows "Roland's" real name. What happened to him was so bizarre and so upsetting that he has never made his name public. Indeed, 50 years after his ordeal, the details of his case still make people shudder with fear.

2   It all began on January 18, 1949. Thirteen-year-old Roland and his parents were living in the sleepy suburban town of Mt. Rainier, Maryland. That night the family heard scratching sounds coming from the walls. The same noises could be heard around the ceiling.

3   Assuming that mice had infested their home, Roland's parents called in an exterminator. But the exterminator found no mice. He found no creatures of any kind. After his examination of the house, the noises continued—in fact, they seemed to grow louder. Soon they were accompanied by squeaking sounds in the hallway.

4   That wasn't all. The family began to notice that kitchen dishes were turning up in strange places around the house. From time to time, they also found that the furniture had been rearranged.

5   Then Roland himself became a target. One night, while trying to sleep, he felt his bed begin to shake. The entire frame shook violently. This continued night after night. Sometimes Roland's blankets were ripped off the bed. When he tried to hang onto them, he was pulled onto the floor along with them.

6   Roland's parents were wild with worry. Suspecting that some sort of evil spirit had invaded their lives, they turned to their local minister, Luther Schulze. Reverend Schulze offered to use the power of prayer to rid the family of its problem.

7   Over the next few weeks, Schulze made many visits to Roland's home. Sometimes he prayed with the whole family, sometimes just with Roland. It didn't do any good. Roland continued to be harassed in his bed, and odd scratching and squeaking sounds continued to be heard throughout the house.

8   Although Schulze did his best to comfort the family, privately he had his doubts about what he saw. He suspected that Roland was playing some kind of prank. Eager to get at the truth, he invited the boy to spend the night at his house. And so, on February 17, the Reverend and Mrs. Schulze prepared twin beds—one for Roland and a second one in the same room for the reverend. That way, Schulze figured, he could keep an eye on Roland all night long.

9   The night began quietly. Sometime after midnight, however, Schulze heard Roland's bed begin to creak. He hurried to the boy's bedside and found the whole bed shaking furiously. Roland's arms were outside the covers, and his body was stretched out straight. There was no way he could be causing the vibrations himself.

10   Quickly Reverend Schulze moved Roland into a heavy armchair. The boy sat

This painting from 1580 shows a priest exorcising a possessed woman.

very still, but soon the chair began to move. It slid backward, slamming into the wall. Then it tipped over on its side, dumping Roland onto the floor.

11   Schulze now realized this was no childhood prank. Something very bad was happening to Roland. Some dark power was at work, and Schulze didn't know how to combat it. Over the next few days, the situation got worse. Back at Roland's house, fruit jumped from its bowl and splattered against the walls. In addition, a strange message appeared scratched in blood across Roland's skin. The message read, "Go to St. Louis!"

12   Schulze urged Roland's parents to take their son to a hospital for a psychological exam. They went to Georgetown University Hospital, but the doctors there were unable to cure Roland or help him in any way. His parents next tried St. Louis Hospital, hoping the choice would please the mysterious force. Doctors there could do nothing, either. In fact, Roland's problems grew more intense. He began to drool and cough uncontrollably. And more bloody scratches appeared on his arms.

13   Finally, Roland's parents turned to exorcism. This is a ritual performed by church officials. It is designed to rid a person of any demon, devil, or other evil spirit that has taken possession of the body. Two different ministers tried to exorcise Roland, but without success. At last, a Jesuit priest was called in. His name was William Bowdern.

14   Bowdern worked with Roland for two solid months. He rarely let the boy out of his sight, even sleeping in the same room with him. Like Reverend Schulze, Father Bowdern saw Roland's bed shake and move across the room. He saw scratches appear on Roland's skin, and he saw objects move of their own accord in Roland's presence.

15   Again and again, Bowdern performed the exorcism rite on the boy. Each exorcism attempt took about 45 minutes. During this time, Roland would go into a kind of trance. He would scream, shout, and curse at the priest. His body seemed to take on superhuman strength, and he would thrash about wildly. He often spat on the priest's face. In addition, he would angrily spout Latin phrases. This last symptom amazed everyone, since Roland had never studied Latin.

16   At last, after 20 exorcisms, the ritual seemed to work. During the last one, Roland remained quiet. There was no more violent cursing, no more rolling around and spitting. Believing he had won the fight for possession of Roland's body and soul, Father Bowdern sent Roland back home. Indeed, from that time on, Roland got better and better. All the problems that had plagued him disappeared. By April, Roland was back to normal.

17   Roland's case had made quite an impression on those around him, though, and they did not quickly forget what they had witnessed. His story was eventually written up in the *New York Times*. There it caught the eye of writer William Peter Blatty. Blatty later used the outline of Roland's story to write his best-selling novel, *The Exorcist*.

If you have been timed while reading this article, enter your reading time below. Then turn to the Words-per-Minute Table on page 133 and look up your reading speed (words per minute). Enter your reading speed on the graph on page 134.

Reading Time: Lesson 10

_____ : _____
Minutes   Seconds

A | Finding the Main Idea

One statement below expresses the main idea of the article. One statement is too general, or too broad. The other statement explains only part of the article; it is too narrow. Label the statements using the following key:

M—Main Idea   **B—Too Broad**   **N—Too Narrow**

_____ 1. An evil spirit scratched bloody messages on 13-year-old Roland's skin.

_____ 2. Exorcism is a ritual performed by church officials to rid the body of evil spirits.

_____ 3. Exorcism was finally used to rid a teenaged boy of an evil spirit that had taken possession of his body.

_____ Score 15 points for a correct M answer.

_____ Score 5 points for each correct B or N answer.

_____ **Total Score:** Finding the Main Idea

B | Recalling Facts

How well do you remember the facts in the article? Put an X in the box next to the answer that correctly completes each statement about the article.

1. Roland's parents called in an exterminator because
   - ☐ a. kitchen dishes were turning up in strange places around the house.
   - ☐ b. they thought mice were responsible for the scratching sounds in their home.
   - ☐ c. the furniture was being rearranged by an unknown force.

2. Reverend Schulze invited Roland to spend the night at his house
   - ☐ a. because he believed the boy was playing a prank.
   - ☐ b. so that he could pray with the boy.
   - ☐ c. because the boy's parents were wild with worry.

3. After the situation got worse, Schulze urged Roland's parents to
   - ☐ a. move to St. Louis.
   - ☐ b. have their son undergo exorcism.
   - ☐ c. take their son to a hospital for a psychological exam.

4. When Father Bowdern performed the first 19 exorcism rites on Roland, the boy would
   - ☐ a. curse, roll around, and spit.
   - ☐ b. scratch his own skin.
   - ☐ c. remain quiet.

5. William Peter Blatty used Roland's story
   - ☐ a. for an article in the *New York Times*.
   - ☐ b. to write *The Exorcist*.
   - ☐ c. to promote the use of exorcism.

Score 5 points for each correct answer.

_____ **Total Score:** Recalling Facts

C Making Inferences

When you combine your own experience and information from a text to draw a conclusion that is not directly stated in that text, you are making an inference. Below are five statements that may or may not be inferences based on information in the article. Label the statements using the following key:

C—Correct Inference   F—Faulty Inference

_____ 1. Roland had no control over what was happening to him.

_____ 2. After the final, successful exorcism, Roland went on to live a normal life.

_____ 3. The doctors who examined Roland could find no physical problem to explain his strange behavior.

_____ 4. Roland had invited the evil spirit to take possession of his body.

_____ 5. Reverend Schulze didn't try as hard as Father Bowdern to help Roland.

Score 5 points for each correct answer.

_____ **Total Score:** Making Inferences

D Using Words Precisely

Each numbered sentence below contains an underlined word or phrase from the article. Following the sentence are three definitions. One definition is closest to the meaning of the underlined word. One definition is opposite or nearly opposite. Label those two definitions using the following key. Do not label the remaining definition.

C—Closest   O—Opposite or Nearly Opposite

1. Indeed, 50 years after his ordeal, the details of his case still make people shudder with fear.

_____ a. cry

_____ b. tremble

_____ c. stay still

2. Roland continued to be harassed in his bed, and odd scratching and squeaking sounds continued to be heard throughout the house.

_____ a. calmed

_____ b. awakened

_____ c. disturbed

3. He suspected that Roland was playing some kind of prank.

_____ a. concert

_____ b. trick

_____ c. sincere behavior

4. During this time, Roland would go into a kind of trance.

_____ a. dreamlike state

_____ b. bad mood

_____ c. condition of being wide awake

5. In addition, he would angrily <u>spout</u> Latin phrases.

_____ a. read

_____ b. speak forcefully

_____ c. speak softly and shyly

_____ Score 3 points for each correct C answer.

_____ Score 2 points for each correct O answer.

_____ **Total Score:** Using Words Precisely

Enter the four total scores in the spaces below, and add them together to find your Reading Comprehension Score. Then record your score on the graph on page 135.

Score	Question Type	Lesson 10
_____	Finding the Main Idea	
_____	Recalling Facts	
_____	Making Inferences	
_____	Using Words Precisely	
_____	**Reading Comprehension Score**	

Author's Approach

Put an X in the box next to the correct answer.

1. The main purpose of the first paragraph is to

☐ a. convey a sense of the fear inspired by Roland's ordeal.

☐ b. inform the reader that Roland is not the subject's real name.

☐ c. tell the reader when Roland's ordeal took place.

2. From the statements below, choose those that you believe the author would agree with.

☐ a. Roland had studied Latin without telling anyone.

☐ b. Roland and his parents didn't want to become rich or famous from their experience.

☐ c. Roland's parents were willing to try anything to cure their son.

3. From the statement "After his [the exterminator's] examination of the house, the noises continued—in fact, they seemed to grow louder," you can conclude that the author wants the reader to think that

☐ a. the exterminator didn't do a good job.

☐ b. Roland's parents got used to the noises.

☐ c. whatever was making the noises was getting stronger and bolder.

4. The author probably wrote this article in order to

☐ a. inform the reader about exorcism.

☐ b. compare the power of prayer with exorcism.

☐ c. inform the reader about what happened to Roland.

_____ Number of correct answers

Record your personal assessment of your work on the Critical Thinking Chart on page 136.

Summarizing and Paraphrasing

Follow the directions provided for question 1. Put an X in the box next to the correct answer for question 2.

1. Look for the important ideas and events in paragraphs 9 and 10. Summarize those paragraphs in one or twoee sentences.

   _____

   _____

   _____

2. Read the statement about the article below. Then read the paraphrase of that statement. Choose the reason that best tells why the paraphrase does not say the same thing as the statement.

   Statement: After reading about Roland's case in the *New York Times*, William Peter Blatty thought the story was so interesting that he used it as the basis for his novel.

   Paraphrase: William Peter Blatty read about Roland's case in the newspaper and thought it was very interesting.

   ☐ a. Paraphrase says too much.

   ☐ b. Paraphrase doesn't say enough.

   ☐ c. Paraphrase doesn't agree with the statement about the article.

   _____ Number of correct answers

   Record your personal assessment of your work on the Critical Thinking Chart on page 136.

Record your personal assessment of your work on the Critical Thinking Chart on page 136.

Critical Thinking

Put an X in the box next to the correct answer for questions 1, 3, and 4. Follow the directions provided for questions 2 and 5.

1. From what the article told about exorcism, you can conclude that it is

   ☐ a. a relatively easy procedure.

   ☐ b. a rare and difficult procedure.

   ☐ c. performed regularly.

2. Choose from the letters below to correctly complete the following statement. Write the letters on the lines.

   In the article, _____ and _____ are different.

   a. Luther Schulze's approach to Roland's problem

   b. William Bowdern's approach to Roland's problems

   c. the approach of the two ministers who tried to exorcise Roland

3. What was the effect of Father Bowdern's exorcism of Roland?

   ☐ a. All the problems that had plagued Roland disappeared.

   ☐ b. Each exorcism attempt took about 45 minutes.

   ☐ c. Father Bowdern worked with Roland for two months.

4. If you were a priest, how could you use the information in the article to perform an exorcism?

   ☐ a. Like Luther Schulze, suggest that the person seek psychological help.

   ☐ b. Like William Bowdern, work closely and intensely with the person who is possessed.

   ☐ c. Like William Peter Blatty, use the possessed person's story to write a best-selling novel.

CRITICAL THINKING

5. In which paragraph did you find the information or details to answer question 3?

_____

_____
_____ Number of correct answers

Record your personal assessment of your work on the Critical Thinking Chart on page 136.

From reading this article, I have learned

_____

_____

_____

_____

Personal Response

If I were the author, I would add

_____

_____

_____

_____

because

_____

_____

_____

CRITICAL THINKING

TRAGEDY AT BORLEY RECTORY

In a quiet valley 60 miles southeast of London, a tragedy was unfolding. A young nun living in a convent had fallen deeply in love with a monk from the nearby Borley monastery. However, church law prohibited both nuns and monks from marrying. The couple decided they had only one option: they would have to elope. They would run away somewhere, give up their religious vows, and settle into life as a happily married couple. With that goal in mind, they made plans for a getaway.

2   The monk convinced a friend at the monastery to help them. So, in the dead of night, the two men slipped into a horse-drawn carriage and then picked up the waiting nun. Before the trio had gotten far, however, they were captured. When the details of their plan were discovered, the two men were promptly hanged. The nun was led to a remote part of the monastery where a wall of bricks was constructed around her, and she was left to die a slow and agonizing death.

3   No one knows the exact date of these events—in fact, no one can prove that the

Borley Rectory was built on the site of a former monastery. The ghost of a nun was seen repeatedly in the early part of the 20th century, often near the gate in this picture.

story is true. But according to legend, the nun, her lover, and their accomplice were killed sometime in the 13th century. Two centuries later, the monastery was destroyed. But although the living abandoned the monastery grounds, many say the spirits of the dead nun and the two monks remained at the site.

4   In 1863, a minister named Henry Bull decided to build a house on the land where the monastery had stood. The building would serve as a rectory, or place of residence for the local clergyman. When the building was completed, Reverend Bull and his large family moved in. But it wasn't long before the family sensed that there was something strange about their new home. They saw stones thrown through the air by some invisible hand. They heard footsteps echoing in empty parts of the house. In 1886, the nursemaid became so alarmed by these events that she gave up her job with the family and moved away.

5   In 1900, Reverend Bull's four daughters were walking in the rear garden of Borley Rectory when they saw a young nun in the path ahead of them. Her head was bowed, and she held a string of beads in her hand. The four sisters stared in disbelief until at last Elsie Bull gathered her courage and stepped forward to make contact with the nun. As she did so, the vision turned and looked at the girls with sad eyes. Then, in an instant, she was gone. An investigator came to the rectory and interviewed each girl separately. Each of them was sure of what she had seen, and each told the same story down to the smallest detail.

6   Over the next 30 years, the nun made several other appearances. One of the Bull sisters saw her again and so did the family cook. Edward Cooper and his wife, who lived next to the rectory, saw the nun many times. The Coopers also saw an old-fashioned carriage drawn by two horses and driven by two men in top hats. As the Coopers watched, the carriage drove into the rectory yard and disappeared. What made the sight so unnerving was that the carriage passed right through hedges and all the other physical obstacles that stood in its path.

7   The strange visions continued even after Reverend Bull died and his family moved away. Fred Cartwright, a carpenter who passed by Borley Rectory every day on his way to work, saw the nun four mornings in a row. Unaware that the place was unoccupied, Cartwright thought nothing of seeing a nun on the rectory grounds. He did notice, however, that she seemed tired. Twice he stopped and tried to wish her good day, but both times she disappeared. He thought perhaps she had run into the building. It was only later that he realized the woman he saw must have been a ghost.

8   As word spread that Borley Rectory was haunted, fewer and fewer clergymen expressed an interest in living there. Twelve ministers turned down the chance to become the town pastor. At last the Reverend Guy Eric Smith agreed to take over the local church and live in the

When Marianne Foyster lived at Borley Rectory, she saw these messages scrawled on the wall.

rectory. Soon after moving in, however, the Smiths had a series of unsettling experiences. They heard footsteps and bells ringing. They saw lights being turned on in empty rooms. Once they heard a woman's voice whispering to them. It began with a low moan, then rose to a scream. "Don't, Carlos, don't," the voice cried.

9   Harry Price, a famous psychic researcher, was called in to examine Borley Rectory. He was stunned by the amount of paranormal activity he found there. He later called it "the most extraordinary and best documented case of haunting" he had ever seen.

10   After the Smiths fled, a new family moved in. They were the Reverend Lionel Foyster, his wife Marianne, and their young daughter. With the Foysters, the ghostly activity reached its peak. Like earlier families, the Foysters heard voices and saw stones flying through the air. But things soon progressed beyond that. Books were hurled from their shelves. Four times Marianne was hit by pottery or other sharp objects. Strange odors permeated the house. Some were pleasant, such as the lavender scent that filled the building one day. But others were foul and noxious.

11   Most frightening were the messages that began to appear all around the house. They were addressed to Marianne. The notes were written in an odd, spidery handwriting and seemed to appear from nowhere. Sometimes the messages were written on little scraps of paper. Sometimes they materialized on the walls of the rectory itself. It was hard to read these so-called "Marianne notes" because the writer often wrote one word on top of another. Some, though, were clearly pleas for help. "Marianne please help get—," read one. Another said, "Marianne help me." And yet another read, "Marianne get help [something illegible] bother me."

12   In 1935, after five years in the rectory, the Foysters moved out. And in 1939, the building burned to the ground. Several years later, researchers found parts of an old skeleton buried beneath the rubble. Analysis showed the bones were those of a young woman who had died long, long ago. Could the skeleton have been that of the murdered nun? No one was sure. But even after the bones were dug up, visitors and passersby often reported seeing a sad and lonely nun on the deserted grounds. Some people heard footsteps, bells, or screams. Others saw lights floating toward them or felt sudden drafts of cold air. The horse-drawn carriage was seen again, once more disintegrating into thin air.

13   Even today, the strange noises and sightings continue. So if you should ever visit the rectory site at Borley, England, be on the lookout for all kinds of strange phenomena. After all, the next person the murdered nun decides to contact could be you. ✿

If you have been timed while reading this article, enter your reading time below. Then turn to the Words-per-Minute Table on page 133 and look up your reading speed (words per minute). Enter your reading speed on the graph on page 134.

Reading Time: Lesson 11

_____ : _____
Minutes   Seconds

Finding the Main Idea

One statement below expresses the main idea of the article. One statement is too general, or too broad. The other statement explains only part of the article; it is too narrow. Label the statements using the following key:

M—Main Idea **B—Too Broad** **N—Too Narrow**

_____ 1. The ghost of a nun put to death for falling in love with a monk was frequently seen at Borley Rectory in England.

_____ 2. Notes believed to have been written by the murdered nun appeared at Borley Rectory.

_____ 3. Some people believed that Borley Rectory was the most haunted house in England.

_____ Score 15 points for a correct M answer.

_____ Score 5 points for each correct B or N answer.

_____ **Total Score:** Finding the Main Idea

 Recalling Facts

How well do you remember the facts in the article? Put an X in the box next to the answer that correctly completes each statement about the article.

1. When the details of the getaway plan were revealed, the nun was

☐ a. promptly hanged.

☐ b. left to die a slow death behind a wall of bricks.

☐ c. led back to the monastery and imprisoned.

2. The first family to live in the newly built Borley Rectory was the

☐ a. Smith family.

☐ b. Foyster family.

☐ c. Bull family.

3. The Coopers were unnerved when they saw a carriage drive through the rectory yard because

☐ a. the nun sitting in the carriage turned to look at them with sad eyes.

☐ b. the carriage passed right through the obstacles in its path.

☐ c. they saw stones thrown through the air by some invisible hand.

4. Many of the notes that appeared all around the rectory were addressed to

☐ a. Marianne Foyster.

☐ b. Elsie Bull.

☐ c. Harry Price.

5. After the rectory burned down, researchers found

☐ a. more mysterious notes.

☐ b. a sad and lonely nun on the deserted grounds.

☐ c. parts of an old skeleton.

Score 5 points for each correct answer.

_____ **Total Score:** Recalling Facts

C | Making Inferences

When you combine your own experience and information from a text to draw a conclusion that is not directly stated in that text, you are making an inference. Below are five statements that may or may not be inferences based on information in the article. Label the statements using the following key:

C—Correct Inference   F—Faulty Inference

_____ 1. The monk and the nun risked everything to be together.

_____ 2. In the 13th century, men and women who became monks and nuns were not allowed to leave their orders.

_____ 3. The Smith family was not frightened by the strange sights and sounds in their home.

_____ 4. Many people think the notes that appeared in the rectory were written by the dead nun.

_____ 5. Researchers have proved that the bones found after the rectory burned down were those of the murdered nun.

Score 5 points for each correct answer.

_____ **Total Score:** Making Inferences

D | Using Words Precisely

Each numbered sentence below contains an underlined word or phrase from the article. Following the sentence are three definitions. One definition is closest to the meaning of the underlined word. One definition is opposite or nearly opposite. Label those two definitions using the following key. Do not label the remaining definition.

C—Closest   O—Opposite or Nearly Opposite

1. However, church law prohibited both nuns and monks from marrying.

_____ a. encouraged

_____ b. prevented

_____ c. ridiculed

2. He was stunned by the amount of paranormal activity he found there.

_____ a. busy

_____ b. ordinary

_____ c. supernatural

3. Strange odors permeated the house.

_____ a. withdrew from

_____ b. penetrated

_____ c. destroyed

4. But others were foul and noxious.

_____ a. toxic

_____ b. colorful

_____ c. healthful

5. The horse-drawn carriage was seen again, once more <u>disintegrating</u> into thin air.

_____ a. flying

_____ b. breaking up

_____ c. coming together

_____ Score 3 points for each correct C answer.

_____ Score 2 points for each correct O answer.

_____ **Total Score:** Using Words Precisely

Enter the four total scores in the spaces below, and add them together to find your Reading Comprehension Score. Then record your score on the graph on page 135.

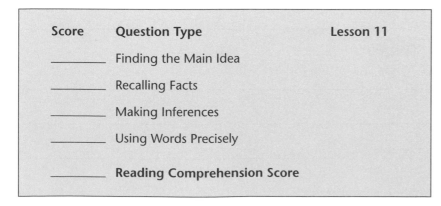

Score	Question Type	Lesson 11
_____	Finding the Main Idea	
_____	Recalling Facts	
_____	Making Inferences	
_____	Using Words Precisely	
_____	**Reading Comprehension Score**	

Author's Approach

Put an X in the box next to the correct answer.

1. The author uses the first paragraph of the article to
   ☐ a. describe the situation the nun and monk faced.
   ☐ b. describe the qualities of the valley.
   ☐ c. compare London and the quiet valley.

2. In this article, "What made the sight so unnerving was that the carriage passed right through hedges and all the other physical obstacles that stood in its path" means
   ☐ a. the carriage destroyed everything in its path.
   ☐ b. the carriage went through objects without touching them.
   ☐ c. the driver of the carriage wasn't very experienced.

3. Choose the statement below that best describes the author's position in paragraph 13.
   ☐ a. The author doesn't believe anyone should visit the rectory site because the murdered nun may try to make contact.
   ☐ b. The author jokingly warns the reader to be careful when visiting the rectory site.
   ☐ c. The author believes that the murdered nun is still haunting the rectory site.

4. The author tells this story mainly by
   ☐ a. focusing solely on the experience of the Bull family.
   ☐ b. comparing the nun with the young women who have lived in the rectory.
   ☐ c. relating the experiences of the families who have lived in the rectory.

_____ Number of correct answers

Record your personal assessment of your work on the Critical Thinking Chart on page 136.

CRITICAL THINKING

Summarizing and Paraphrasing

Put an X in the box next to the correct answer.

1. Below are summaries of the article. Choose the summary that says all the most important things about the article but in the fewest words.

☐ a. A monk and a nun who had fallen in love were caught trying to run away and were put to death. Witnesses have reported seeing apparitions and other strange things on the site where the nun was murdered.

☐ b. After a nun, a monk, and their accomplice were caught trying to escape from a monastery, the trio were put to death.

☐ c. After a nun and a monk fell in love, an accomplice helped them run away from a monastery. The trio were caught, however, and put to death. The men were hanged, and the nun was walled up in the monastery.

2. Choose the sentence that correctly restates the following sentence from the article:

"The four sisters stared in disbelief until at last Elsie Bull gathered her courage and stepped forward to make contact with the nun."

☐ a. The four sisters couldn't believe it when Elsie touched the nun.

☐ b. The sisters stared at Elsie until she stepped on the nun.

☐ c. The sisters stood starting at the nun until Elsie bravely stepped up to communicate with the nun.

_____ Number of correct answers

Record your personal assessment of your work on the Critical Thinking Chart on page 136.

Critical Thinking

Follow the directions provided for questions 1 and 2. Put an X in the box next to the correct answer for questions 3 and 4.

1. For each statement below, write O if it expresses an opinion and write F if it expresses a fact.

_____ a. It is almost impossible to believe that spirits of the dead nun and the two monks haunt the site of the old monastery.

_____ b. Notes addressed to Marianne were found in the rectory when the Foyster family lived there.

_____ c. Anyone who builds a home over the site of a tragedy is foolish.

2. Using what is told about the Bull family and the Foyster family in the article, name three ways the Bulls' experiences in the rectory are similar to and three ways they are different from those of the Foyster family. Cite the paragraph number(s) where you found details in the article to support your conclusions.

Similarities

_____

_____

_____

Differences

_____

_____

_____

3. What caused the Bulls' nursemaid to give up her job ?

☐ a. She heard a woman's voice whispering and then screaming at her.

☐ b. A vision turned and looked at her with sad eyes.

☐ c. The strange events at the rectory frightened her.

4. Of the following theme categories, which would this story fit into?

☐ a. Don't be guided by your emotions.

☐ b. There is life after death.

☐ c. There's no place like home.

_____ Number of correct answers

Record your personal assessment of your work on the Critical Thinking Chart on page 136.

Personal Response

What would you have done if the apparition had turned and looked at you?

_____

_____

_____

_____

Self-Assessment

One good question about this article that was not asked would be

_____

_____

_____

_____

and the answer is

_____

_____

_____

_____

_____

CRITICAL THINKING

SARAH'S GHOST HOUSE
An Architectural Fun House

The Winchester Mystery House in San Jose, California. Inset: Mrs. Sarah Winchester lived as a recluse, and this is the only known photo of her.

In 1862 Sarah Pardee had everything to look forward to. That year she married William Wirt Winchester, heir to the Winchester rifle fortune. (At that time the Winchester rifle was the most famous rifle in the world.) Sarah and her husband moved to a large, lovely home in New Haven, Connecticut. Soon they had a baby girl, whom they named Annie Pardee. Then tragedy struck. Just one month after her birth, baby Annie died from a mysterious illness. A few short months later, William also died.

2   Sarah was devastated. She withdrew into her home and refused to see anyone. She thought only of her double tragedy, and became convinced that the Winchesters were cursed. The rifle that bore their name had been responsible for the deaths of thousands. Sarah felt that the spirits of those dead people were seeking revenge.

3   Sarah had always been interested in the occult—the mysteries of the spirit world. Now she became obsessed with it. Hoping to make contact with her baby and her husband, Sarah invited mediums into her home. Mediums claim that they

can contact the dead through meetings called séances. None of the mediums, however, was able to get through to William or to baby Annie.

4   Then Sarah learned of a medium named Adam Coons, who lived in Boston. People assured her that if anyone could make contact with the dead, he could. Without telling him who she was, Sarah visited Coons, and he agreed to stage a séance for her.

5   During the séance, Coons told Sarah that the spirit of her late husband was standing beside her. "Tell him that I miss him desperately," she said. "He wants you to know that he will always be with you," Coons replied. Then he gave Sarah a chilling warning. "Unless you do something in their memory, the ghosts of those who have been killed by Winchester rifles will haunt you forever."

6   "But what can I do?" Sarah pleaded. Coons told her that she was to move to the West and buy a house that her husband's spirit would pick out. Then she was to enlarge the house, making sure it had enough room to house those spirits. As long as she continued to build on to the house, Sarah was told, she would remain alive and unharmed.

7   Coons had not been told Sarah's identity. How, then, did he know about her husband's death and the family's connection to the Winchester rifle? Sarah was convinced that the ghost of her husband had spoken through the medium. She set out to follow his instructions.

8   In 1884 Sarah sold her home in New Haven and traveled to California. There, following what she later said was William's advice, she bought an eight-room house on 44 acres of land in San Jose, a city about 50 miles south of San Francisco.

9   She set about enlarging the house. Luckily, money was no problem. Sarah had inherited William's fortune—about 20 million dollars. She also received about 1,000 dollars a day from the Winchester Arms Company.

10   Sarah hired a small army of workers. There were 18 carpenters, 12 gardeners, and countless plumbers, plasterers, stonemasons, and painters. For the next 38 years, they worked around the clock, every day, all year long. The hammering and sawing never ceased.

11   Sarah herself took charge of every detail of the work. Each morning she gave the head workman the plans she had sketched on an old envelope or paper bag the night before. And each night she would seek the opinions of the ghosts that she said inhabited the house. More often than not, it seems, they did not like her plans, or they would change their minds about what they wanted.

12   The result was that walls built one day would be torn down the next. Windows would be installed only to be blocked up. Doors were added, then taken out, and so on. One worker spent 33 years doing nothing but laying fancy wooden floors and then tearing them up!

13   As each new room was completed, Sarah would furnish it or fill it with treasures that would later be used to furnish other rooms. Some rooms held rolls of costly French wallpapers. Others held stacks of paintings. Still others were crammed with ornaments of copper, gold, and silver.

14   Railroad cars filled with European and Asian riches for the mansion arrived almost daily at the San Jose depot. For small items, Sarah shopped locally. She drove one of her two automobiles—both two-tone lavender and yellow Pierce Arrows. When she arrived at a store, she never got out of the car. No matter, for the eager shopkeepers gladly brought items out for her approval.

15   Sarah spent almost as much time planning the grounds as she did the house. She ordered her gardeners to plant a six-foot-high cypress hedge around the

A stairway to nowhere in Winchester House

entire estate. They also planted exotic gardens and orchards. Elaborate fountains spewed water 24 hours a day. And paths wound through this wonderland in a confusing maze.

16   In honor of the many Native Americans killed by white armies using Winchester rifles, Sarah had a statue sculpted for the garden. It depicted Chief Little Fawn shooting arrows.

17   In the end, the house covered six acres. It contained 160 rooms, 47 fireplaces, and 40 staircases. There were 10,000 windows, 52 skylights, 467 doorways, 6 kitchens, a formal dining room, and a grand ballroom. In all, Sarah spent five million dollars on her ghost house.

18   Some details of the house are quite odd. It has five heating systems and three elevators. Secret passageways are everywhere, but many lead to blank walls. Many of the staircases lead nowhere. One has 40 steps, each only two inches high! One room has nothing but trap doors. Another has a skylight—in the floor. On the second floor, some of the doors open onto thin air.

19   Sarah was obsessed by the number 13. Each light fixture has 13 globes. Some staircases have 13 steps. The house has 13 bathrooms, and Sarah's bathroom has 13 windows.

20   The house took up Sarah's every waking moment. The work was all she had, for she never invited anyone into the house. Even a president was turned away from the door. In 1903 President Theodore Roosevelt dropped by for a visit but was told by a servant that "the house was not open to strangers." He never did get in.

21   But perhaps Sarah was not alone in her rambling mansion. In her later years, it was said that every night, when the tower bell tolled midnight, organ music wafted from the house. It could not have been Sarah playing, for her fingers had grown so stiff with age that she could hardly hold a pencil.

22   Clearly, Sarah herself believed that she had ghostly guests, for she dined with them each evening. Servants would set 13 places at the table, heap each plate with food, and fill the crystal goblets with the finest wines. That was Sarah's nightly offering to any spirits who cared to dine. "Good evening," she would say. "I am pleased that you have come to share my food and my house. Please enjoy yourselves." Early each morning, the servants would clear the dining room. They never revealed whether the food and wine had been touched.

23   Outwardly, Sarah was the perfect hostess, but secretly she was terrified of the ghosts. So that they wouldn't find her when she was sleeping, she slept in a different room each night.

24   Sarah Winchester devoted her life to making amends to those who had been killed by Winchester rifles. But the house she labored over was not enough to save her, despite Adam Coons's promise that she would not die as long as she kept building. She died there in 1922, at the age of 85. At the time of her death, there was enough material on the site to continue building for another 38 years.

25   Sarah left no will, so the furnishings were put up for auction. It took six large vans working eight hours a day for six weeks to haul off all her belongings. A year later the house itself was sold. The new owners opened it to visitors, charging a fee for the opportunity to wander through it. On May 13, 1974, the Winchester House was designated a California Historical Landmark.

26   Today visitors marvel at the strange, sprawling building. Frequent visitors say that the house is larger today than it was when Sarah died. Since there were no plans for the house, no blueprints, there is no proof. Still, people insist that new rooms have been added. Could Sarah still be trying to make amends? Some people think so. But whatever the case, the Winchester House is like no other house on earth—an architectural fun house built for the comfort of invisible residents. 🍃

If you have been timed while reading this article, enter your reading time below. Then turn to the Words-per-Minute Table on page 133 and look up your reading speed (words per minute). Enter your reading speed on the graph on page 134.

Reading Time: Lesson 12

_____ : _____
Minutes   *Seconds*

A Finding the Main Idea

One statement below expresses the main idea of the article. One statement is too general, or too broad. The other statement explains only part of the article; it is too narrow. Label the statements using the following key:

M—Main Idea　　　**B—Too Broad**　　　**N—Too Narrow**

_____　1. The house that Sarah Winchester built in Northern California had 47 fireplaces and 40 staircases.

_____　2. Sarah Winchester spent most of her life trying to make amends for the deaths of people killed by Winchester rifles.

_____　3. Sarah Winchester built a huge, rambling puzzle of a house for the ghosts of the people killed by Winchester rifles.

_____　Score 15 points for a correct M answer.

_____　Score 5 points for each correct B or N answer.

_____　**Total Score:** Finding the Main Idea

B Recalling Facts

How well do you remember the facts in the article? Put an X in the box next to the answer that correctly completes each statement about the article.

1. Sarah Winchester moved to San Jose, California, from
   - ☐ a. Boston, Massachusetts.
   - ☐ b. San Francisco, California.
   - ☐ c. New Haven, Connecticut.

2. All her life, Sarah had been interested in
   - ☐ a. rifles.
   - ☐ b. the occult.
   - ☐ c. building a great mansion.

3. Sarah went to mediums in order to
   - ☐ a. try to contact her dead husband and baby.
   - ☐ b. ask the spirits of people killed by Winchester rifles how she might make amends to them.
   - ☐ c. find out what she should do with her life.

4. Sarah started adding to her mansion in the
   - ☐ a. early 1900s.
   - ☐ b. late 1880s.
   - ☐ c. 1840s.

5. Sarah's house contained
   - ☐ a. 725 rooms.
   - ☐ b. 467 rooms.
   - ☐ c. 160 rooms.

Score 5 points for each correct answer.

_____　**Total Score:** Recalling Facts

C Making Inferences

When you combine your own experience and information from a text to draw a conclusion that is not directly stated in that text, you are making an inference. Below are five statements that may or may not be inferences based on information in the article. Label the statements using the following key:

C—Correct Inference   F—Faulty Inference

_____ 1. William Winchester was an evil man.

_____ 2. Adam Coons continued to advise Sarah Winchester throughout her life.

_____ 3. If William and Annie had not died, Sarah would not have built her ghost house.

_____ 4. The materials that were left on the site when Sarah died were used to continue adding to the house.

_____ 5. Sarah's servants must have had interesting stories to tell.

Score 5 points for each correct answer.

_____ **Total Score:** Making Inferences

D Using Words Precisely

Each numbered sentence below contains an underlined word or phrase from the article. Following the sentence are three definitions. One definition is closest to the meaning of the underlined word. One definition is opposite or nearly opposite. Label those two definitions using the following key. Do not label the remaining definition.

C—Closest   O—Opposite or Nearly Opposite

1. Now she became <u>obsessed</u> with it.

_____ a. confused

_____ b. totally absorbed

_____ c. uninterested

2. Elaborate fountains <u>spewed</u> water 24 hours a day.

_____ a. shot forth

_____ b. pulled in

_____ c. leaked

3. It <u>depicted</u> Chief Little Fawn shooting arrows.

_____ a. pictured

_____ b. belonged to

_____ c. hid

4. Sarah Winchester devoted her life to <u>making amends to</u> those who had been killed by Winchester rifles.

_____ a. apologizing to

_____ b. praying for

_____ c. further offending

5. But the house she labored over was not enough to save her, <u>despite</u> Adam Coons's promise that she would not die as long as she kept building.

_____ a. without

_____ b. regardless of

_____ c. because of

_____ Score 3 points for each correct C answer.

_____ Score 2 points for each correct O answer.

_____ **Total Score:** Using Words Precisely

Enter the four total scores in the spaces below, and add them together to find your Reading Comprehension Score. Then record your score on the graph on page 135.

Score	Question Type	Lesson 12
_____	Finding the Main Idea	
_____	Recalling Facts	
_____	Making Inferences	
_____	Using Words Precisely	
_____	**Reading Comprehension Score**	

Author's Approach

Put an X in the box next to the correct answer.

1. Which of the following statements from the article best describes Sarah Winchester?

☐ a. "In 1862 Sarah Pardee had everything to look forward to."

☐ b. "She drove one of her two automobiles—both two-tone lavender and yellow Pierce Arrows."

☐ c. "Sarah had always been interested in the occult—the mysteries of the spirit world."

2. From the statement "In 1903 President Theodore Roosevelt dropped by for a visit but was told by a servant that 'the house was not open to strangers,'" you can conclude that the author wants the reader to think that Sarah

☐ a. didn't like the President.

☐ b. was very eccentric and solitary.

☐ c. didn't understand politics.

3. Choose the statement below that is the weakest argument for claiming that, even after death, Sarah is trying to make amends to those killed by Winchester rifles.

☐ a. Frequent visitors to the house say that it is larger today than it was when Sarah died.

☐ b. Some people insist that new rooms have been added since Sarah's death.

☐ c. Since there were no blueprints, no one is sure how big the house was when Sarah died.

4. The author probably wrote this article in order to

☐ a.   tell the reader about Sarah Winchester and her house.

☐ b.   convey a tragic mood.

☐ c.   express an opinion about the harm done by Winchester rifles.

_____ Number of correct answers

Record your personal assessment of your work on the Critical Thinking Chart on page 136.

Summarizing and Paraphrasing

Follow the directions provided for question 1. Put an X in the box next to the correct answer for question 2.

1. Look for the important ideas and events in paragraphs 5 and 6. Summarize those paragraphs in one or two sentences.

_____

_____

_____

2. Choose the best one-sentence paraphrase for the following sentence from the article:

"In her later years, it was said that every night, when the tower bell tolled midnight, organ music wafted from the house."

☐ a.   Every night, Sarah played the organ so loud that her neighbors could hear it.

☐ b.   After Sarah died, people said that organ music drifted from the tower at midnight.

☐ c.   When Sarah got older, people claimed that every night at midnight, the sounds of organ music drifted from the house.

_____ Number of correct answers

Record your personal assessment of your work on the Critical Thinking Chart on page 136.

Critical Thinking

Put an X in the box next to the correct answer for questions 1, 2, and 5. Follow the directions provided for questions 3 and 4.

1. Which of the following statements from the article is an opinion rather than a fact?

☐ a.   "Some details of the house are quite odd."

☐ b.   "Just one month after her birth, baby Annie died from a mysterious illness."

☐ c.   "In 1884 Sarah sold her home in New Haven and traveled to California."

CRITICAL THINKING

2. From the article, you can predict that if Sarah Winchester had not consulted Adam Coons,

☐ a. she would have lost interest in the occult.

☐ b. she would not have moved to California.

☐ c. her husband's ghost would have spoken directly to Sarah.

3. Choose from the letters below to correctly complete the following statement. Write the letters on the lines.

On the positive side, _____, but on the negative side _____.

a. Sarah attached special importance to the number 13

b. Sarah remained frightened of the ghosts she believed still haunted her

c. Sarah created a fascinating house

4. Think about cause-effect relationships in the article. Fill in the blanks in the cause-effect chart, drawing from the letters below.

Cause	Effect
The ghosts didn't like Sarah's plans.	_____
Sarah's husband and child died.	_____
_____	She slept in a different bedroom every night.

a. Sarah was terrified of the ghosts that inhabited her house.

b. Sarah became convinced that the Winchesters were cursed.

c. Work had to be torn down and redone.

5. What did you have to do to answer question 1?

☐ a. find an opinion (what someone thinks about something)

☐ b. find a summary (synthesized information)

☐ c. find a cause (why something happened)

_____ Number of correct answers

Record your personal assessment of your work on the Critical Thinking Chart on page 136.

Personal Response

If you could ask the author of the article one question, what would it be?

_____

_____

_____

_____

Self-Assessment

I was confused on question #_____ in section _____ because

_____

_____

_____

_____

LESSON 13

A TOWER FULL OF GHOSTS

Late one night, a guard rushed into the guardroom at the Tower of London, white with fear. He tried to shout, but all he could manage was a hoarse whisper. "Man in cloak! Man in cloak!" he gasped desperately. When the other sentries finally managed to calm him down, the guard told his story. He had been out patrolling the Tower grounds as usual when he saw a cloaked figure step from the shadows. Ready for trouble, the guard drew closer to confront the intruder. But as he did so, he saw something that made his blood run cold. The man in the cloak had no head.

2   This incident, which occurred in the late 1960s, was by no means the first time a ghost had been seen at the Tower of London. Over the years, there have been countless reports of strange phenomena on these grounds. Some people have expressed surprise that a major landmark like the Tower of London could be haunted. But when you consider the Tower's history, it makes sense. Some experts say that hauntings occur when people are unjustly or prematurely killed.

Anne Boleyn, second wife of Henry VIII, was imprisoned in the Tower of London on charges of treason and beheaded in 1536. It is said that her ghost haunts the Tower.

Since the victims' spirits are not ready to leave this world, they may linger at the site where they last lived. If that is the case, the Tower of London is the perfect place to find ghosts. It was here that hundreds of people—many of them innocent—were imprisoned, tortured, and killed.

3   The Tower of London was built over 900 years ago, when William the Conqueror had a huge stone tower erected to serve as a fort and a palace. Over time, other kings enlarged the living quarters and added a chapel. They also put up buildings that could be used as courthouses, cells, and torture chambers. By the Middle Ages, using the Tower as a prison had become very popular with English kings. Deep within its walls, prisoners could be tortured in any number of ways. Those who did not confess to crimes were killed. Those who did confess were often killed anyway.

4   For a time, executions took place almost every day. Victims were beheaded, hanged, burned, or stabbed. Many of these victims were poor. But the rich and powerful were sometimes targeted, as well. In 1536, Henry VIII sent his second wife, Anne Boleyn, to the Tower. Angry that she had not been able to produce a male heir, he made up false charges against her. After

she was convicted, Anne was beheaded in front of the Tower chapel. Other important figures who were killed in the Tower include 17-year-old Lady Jane Grey, Sir Walter Raleigh, and the Countess of Salisbury.

5   The last execution in the Tower took place during World War II, when a spy was shot to death. Even before that final killing, though, ghosts had begun to appear on the premises. Some of the ghosts are impossible to identify. They often appear in medieval clothes, sometimes sobbing or groaning in pain in their torture chambers. In 1994, a woman named Shannon John took a photograph of the Tower gate. When the picture was developed, she was shocked to see an arm, clothed in a 16th-century tunic, in the right hand corner. No one knows where the arm came from, but John is convinced it belongs to a spirit. "It's a ghost," she says. "There were only two people there, me and a friend, and the arm doesn't belong to either of us."

6   Some of the Tower ghosts are not so anonymous. Consider the apparition seen by a captain at the Tower. As one of the guards who marched around the Tower grounds at night, the captain was accustomed to the dreary atmosphere that permeates the place. But he was not

prepared to see a light on in the Tower chapel late one night.

7   "What's the meaning of that?" he asked one of the sentries. "Surely it's too late an hour for any service."

8   The sentry confirmed that no church service had been scheduled in the chapel. "But I've often see that light and stranger

The Tower of London as it probably looked about the time that Anne Boleyn was beheaded

things too," the sentry said. "So have the other night sentries...."

9   Determined to investigate, the captain had a ladder brought to him. Placing it against one of the chapel windows, he scrambled up and peered inside. What he saw amazed and frightened him. The chapel was aglow with a bluish light. Down the center aisle strode a group of men and women, all dressed in medieval clothes. Leading them was the unmistakable figure of the dead Queen Anne Boleyn. She led the group up and down the aisles of the chapel several times. Then, as the captain watched, she and all the others suddenly vanished. At the same time, the bluish light went out, and the chapel returned to darkness.

10   Even more eerie is the ghost of the 70-year-old Countess of Salisbury. The Countess was killed in the Tower in 1541. Innocent of the charges against her, she would not cooperate with the executioner. She refused to bend over and place her head on the chopping block. Instead, she announced that if the axman wanted her head, he would have to come get it. So saying, she began to run. The executioner hurried after her, swinging his ax wildly. Three times he nicked her. With his fourth attempt, he struck her neck but did not sever her head. Only on the fifth blow did he manage to behead the old lady.

11   According to some, this grisly scene is played out in ghostly form on May 27th, the anniversary of the Countess's death. Witnesses have reported seeing the ghastly event every year since the 1950s.

12   Lady Jane Grey's ghost also makes her appearance on the anniversary of her death. In 1957, a sentry noticed a white light on the roof of the Tower. As he watched, the light assumed the shape of the young Lady Jane. Not quite trusting his own senses, the sentry called to a second guard. This second man, too, saw the ghostly figure.

13   Some people don't believe the reports of ghosts at the Tower of London. But Geoffrey Abbott believes them. Abbott used to work as a watchman at the Tower. He has written several books about the ghosts that appear there. Abbott points out that many of the sightings come from guards and watchmen. These are people who are paid to make accurate observations. "You can't discount people like that," Abbott says. "They're not the sort to get hoaxes or imagine things."

If you have been timed while reading this article, enter your reading time below. Then turn to the Words-per-Minute Table on page 133 and look up your reading speed (words per minute). Enter your reading speed on the graph on page 134.

Reading Time: **Lesson 13**

_____ : _____
Minutes   Seconds

Finding the Main Idea

One statement below expresses the main idea of the article. One statement is too general, or too broad. The other statement explains only part of the article; it is too narrow. Label the statements using the following key:

M—Main Idea   B—Too Broad   N—Too Narrow

_____ 1. A guard at the Tower of London saw the ghost of Anne Boleyn in the Tower chapel.

_____ 2. Some people say that hauntings occur at places where people were unjustly or prematurely killed.

_____ 3. Many witnesses have seen the ghosts of people, both well known and unidentified, who were put to death in the Tower of London.

_____ Score 15 points for a correct M answer.

_____ Score 5 points for each correct B or N answer.

_____ **Total Score:** Finding the Main Idea

 Recalling Facts

How well do you remember the facts in the article? Put an X in the box next to the answer that correctly completes each statement about the article.

1. A Tower guard in the late 1960s was white with fear after seeing
   ☐ a. an intruder on the grounds.
   ☐ b. a sobbing woman in medieval clothing.
   ☐ c. a headless man.

2. The Tower of London was built during the reign of
   ☐ a. William the Conqueror.
   ☐ b. Henry VIII.
   ☐ c. Walter Raleigh.

3. An arm clothed in a 16th-century tunic appeared in a photo taken by
   ☐ a. Shannon John.
   ☐ b. Geoffrey Abbott.
   ☐ c. a spy during World War II.

4. Looking through one of the Tower chapel windows, a guard saw
   ☐ a. the execution of the Countess of Salisbury.
   ☐ b. the ghosts of Anne Boleyn and others marching up and down the aisles.
   ☐ c. a white light, which assumed the form of Lady Jane Grey.

5. When asked to place her head on the chopping block, the Countess of Salisbury
   ☐ a. suddenly vanished.
   ☐ b. refused to cooperate.
   ☐ c. ran away and eventually escaped.

Score 5 points for each correct answer.

_____ **Total Score:** Recalling Facts

C Making Inferences

When you combine your own experience and information from a text to draw a conclusion that is not directly stated in that text, you are making an inference. Below are five statements that may or may not be inferences based on information in the article. Label the statements using the following key:

C—Correct Inference   F—Faulty Inference

_____ 1. The guards who patrol the grounds at the Tower of London have wild imaginations.

_____ 2. Henry VIII wanted a son who would inherit his throne when he died.

_____ 3. The Countess of Salisbury was a timid old woman who did what she was told.

_____ 4. Ghost sightings have not been reported since the late 1960s.

_____ 5. The Tower of London was the site of great cruelty.

Score 5 points for each correct answer.

_____ **Total Score:** Making Inferences

D Using Words Precisely

Each numbered sentence below contains an underlined word or phrase from the article. Following the sentence are three definitions. One definition is closest to the meaning of the underlined word. One definition is opposite or nearly opposite. Label those two definitions using the following key. Do not label the remaining definition.

C—Closest   O—Opposite or Nearly Opposite

1. He tried to shout, but all he could manage was a hoarse whisper.

_____ a. angry

_____ b. husky and harsh

_____ c. musical and pleasing

2. Some of the Tower ghosts are not so anonymous.

_____ a. recognized

_____ b. frightening

_____ c. unidentified

3. Down the center aisle strode a group of men and women, all dressed in medieval clothes.

_____ a. stood still

_____ b. marched

_____ c. appeared

4. With his fourth attempt, he struck her neck but did not sever her head.

_____ a. disconnect

_____ b. attach

_____ c. see

5. Witnesses have reported seeing the <u>ghastly</u> event every year since the 1950s.

_____ a. annual

_____ b. appealing

_____ c. dreadful

_____ Score 3 points for each correct C answer.

_____ Score 2 points for each correct O answer.

_____ **Total Score:** Using Words Precisely

Enter the four total scores in the spaces below, and add them together to find your Reading Comprehension Score. Then record your score on the graph on page 135.

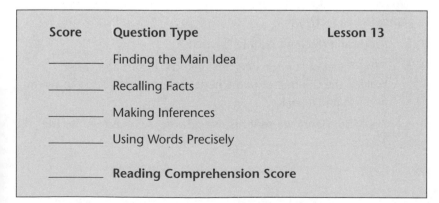

Score	Question Type	Lesson 13
_____	Finding the Main Idea	
_____	Recalling Facts	
_____	Making Inferences	
_____	Using Words Precisely	
_____	**Reading Comprehension Score**	

Author's Approach

Put an X in the box next to the correct answer.

1. The author uses the first paragraph of the article to

☐ a. inform the reader about guards at the Tower of London.

☐ b. describe one ghostly incident at the Tower.

☐ c. entertain the reader with tales of ghosts at the Tower.

2. What does the author imply by saying "Those who did confess were often killed anyway"?

☐ a. Most of the prisoners in the Tower of London deserved to die.

☐ b. People imprisoned in the Tower should never have confessed.

☐ c. Prisoners in the Tower of London were shown little justice or mercy.

3. Choose the statement below that best describes the author's position in paragraph 2.

☐ a. The author is surprised that a famous landmark like the Tower of London is thought to be haunted.

☐ b. Ghosts are more likely to appear in places where people were unjustly killed.

☐ c. If ghosts do exist, the Tower of London would be a logical place to look for them since many acts of cruelty took place there.

4. The author tells this story mainly by

☐ a. retelling one guard's personal experiences at the Tower of London.

☐ b. comparing haunted landmarks in London.

☐ c. telling different stories about ghosts that haunt the Tower of London.

_____ Number of correct answers

Record your personal assessment of your work on the Critical Thinking Chart on page 136.

Summarizing and Paraphrasing

Follow the directions provided for questions 1 and 2. Put an X in the box next to the correct answer for question 3.

1. Complete the following one-sentence summary of the article using the lettered phrases from the phrase bank below. Write the letters on the lines.

Phrase Bank:
a. who some of the more famous ghosts are
b. a description of the Tower's bloody history
c. one man's opinion about the reliability of the witnesses who have seen the ghosts

After a short introduction, the article about the ghosts in the Tower of London begins with _____, goes on to explain _____, and ends with _____.

2. Reread paragraph 10 in the article. Below, write a summary of the paragraph in no more than 25 words.

_____

_____

_____

_____

Reread your summary and decide whether it covers the important ideas in the paragraph. Next, decide how to shorten the summary to 15 words or less without leaving out any essential information. Write this summary below.

_____

_____

3. Choose the best one-sentence paraphrase for the following sentence from the article:

"As one of the guards who marched around the Tower grounds at night, the captain was accustomed to the dreary atmosphere that permeates the place."

☐ a. As he walked around the grounds, the captain felt depressed by the Tower's atmosphere.

☐ b. The captain was used to the Tower's gloomy atmosphere.

☐ c. The captain was used to walking around the Tower grounds at night.

_____ Number of correct answers

Record your personal assessment of your work on the Critical Thinking Chart on page 136.

Critical Thinking

Put an X in the box next to the correct answer for questions 1 and 2. Follow the directions provided for questions 3 and 4.

1. Which of the following statements from the article is an opinion rather than a fact?

☐ a. "You can't discount people like that."

☐ b. "The Tower of London was built over 900 years ago, when William the Conqueror had a huge stone tower erected to serve as a fort and a palace."

☐ c. "In 1536, Henry VIII sent his second wife, Anne Boleyn, to the Tower."

CRITICAL THINKING

2. From the events in the article, you can predict that the following will happen next:

☐ a. The Tower of London will close to the public because of its reputation as a haunted site.

☐ b. People will continue to report seeing the Countess of Salisbury's ghost on May 27th.

☐ c. The English monarchy will once again use the Tower for executions.

3. Using what is told about the Countess of Salisbury and Lady Jane Grey in the article, name three ways the Countess of Salisbury is similar to and three ways she is different from Lady Jane Grey. Cite the paragraph number(s) where you found details in the article to support your conclusions.

Similarities

_____

_____

_____

Differences

_____

_____

_____

4. Choose from the letters below to correctly complete the following statement. Write the letters on the lines.

According to the article, _____ caused Henry VIII to _____, and the effect was _____.

a. bring false charges against her

b. Anne Boleyn's inability to produce a son

c. she was beheaded in front of the Tower chapel

_____ Number of correct answers

Record your personal assessment of your work on the Critical Thinking Chart on page 136.

Personal Response

Begin the first 5–8 sentences of your own article about seeing a ghost that haunts a public building. Your story may include realistic details along with imagined events.

_____

_____

_____

_____

_____

_____

Self-Assessment

Before reading this article, I already knew

_____

_____

_____

_____

CRITICAL THINKING

HARVEY OF FORT SAM HOUSTON

The Hacienda Recreation Center at Fort Sam Houston, San Antonio, Texas, is said to be haunted by a ghost known as Harvey.

Windows opening and doors slamming for no apparent reason. Footsteps crunching in empty rooms. Music drifting out of a ceiling. The carriage of a typewriter moving back and forth as if driven by some unseen hand. Some 20 years ago, at Service Club Number 2 at the U.S. Army Medical Training Center in Fort Sam Houston, Texas, such strange happenings were almost taken for granted. The people who worked in the club would just shrug and say, "Harvey's at it again."

2   The Service Club was a social center for enlisted soldiers and their families, and they welcomed all manner of guests. Harvey was, without a doubt, the most unusual. You see, Harvey was a ghost. How he (or "it") came by the name Harvey is a mystery.

3   Those who encountered Harvey did not jump to the conclusion that they were dealing with a ghost. They were more sensible than that. No, they began by investigating every possible normal explanation for the strange events that took place. Finally, a ghost seemed to be the only plausible explanation.

4   Harvey was not malicious, as some ghosts are, but he could make quite a nuisance of himself. When Phyllis Boyes was director of the service club, in 1967 and 1968, Harvey's habit of opening windows that had been locked for the night used to drive her crazy.

5   "In the first place," Ms. Boyes explained, "when a building is left open here…it means the Military Police call you whenever they discover it, no matter what time of night. You then have to return to the building to check it out and make sure there hasn't been a break-in. This, at some unpleasant hour like two o'clock in the morning, can be quite irritating. So closing up the place and securing it is very important. This is why I got so put out with the young men to whom I entrusted this job. They assured me that they had carefully locked up in each case, but as they would leave the building, they would look back and see a window open. This happened time and time again, and I insisted the men were being very careless. Finally, we set up a system where one fellow would close up the building and then two of us would go around checking on him. We would then leave, vowing that all the windows and doors were thoroughly locked. We might still, as like as not, find an upstairs window open when we looked back."

6   Army First Sergeant Louis Milligan confirmed Ms. Boyes's statement. On more than one occasion he locked all the windows in the building, only to find one or more open when he got outside and looked around.

7   Could the locks have been faulty? Were there broken sashes that allowed the windows to slip down by themselves? No, in both cases. Each window had been securely bolted, so the windows could not possibly have been opened unless someone had released the bolts.

8   Harvey made his presence known in other ways too. Sometimes he would walk around noisily, for his footsteps were frequently heard on the second floor of the Service Club. But whenever the upstairs rooms were searched, they were found to be empty. There didn't seem to be any way that a person could have left the building without being noticed, either, unless, of course, that "someone" happened to be a ghost!

9   On hearing the footsteps, one young soldier, who didn't believe in spirits, demanded that Harvey prove his existence. "Harvey, if you're up there, you got to make me know it," he demanded. A few minutes later, the young soldier heard the sound of a door slamming directly behind him. He whirled around, only to find the door wide open!

10   Then there was the musical incident. Sergeant Milligan described what happened when he and a worker were closing up the club one evening: "We had fastened up everything securely and were getting ready to leave. Then, just as we were in the lobby, we heard this beautiful music. It seemed to be coming out of the ceiling." Both men clearly heard the

Harvey allegedly opens this window at the Hacienda Recreation Center.

music, which they said sounded as though it was made by a flute. When Sergeant Milligan went upstairs to investigate the source of the music, the sound stopped. When he went back down the stairs, it started up again.

11 Was there some natural cause for the music? Sergeant Milligan was certain the building was empty. But might a radio have been left on in some office? The offices were checked, but all the radios were off. Could a trickster have been hiding somewhere in the building? The janitors, who were intimately familiar with all the nooks and crannies of the building, were asked to check every possible hiding place. No one was ever discovered.

12 Shortly after the music episode, a typewriter apparently went into action on its own. There were two men in the room at the time. Both had their backs to the typewriter when they suddenly heard the carriage slide across the machine so forcefully that the end-of-line bell rang. Neither soldier could have moved the carriage without the other's being aware of it.

13 Another witness to Harvey's antics claimed to have heard the characteristic sounds of a table tennis game being played. "It went 'ping, pong, pong,'" she said, "but no one else was in the room." Could Harvey have invited a fellow ghost in for a night of recreation?

14 Yet another person claimed to have heard Harvey clear his throat. That person was putting some food back into a refrigerator when she heard someone "harrumph" right behind her. Although she reminded herself that ghosts do not have throats to clear, she could find no one else in the building.

15 Not all of Harvey's antics were confined to Service Club Number 2. Sergeant Milligan related a story about his electric saw, which disappeared from his home not far from the club. "I was doing some work at home one Saturday and decided to use the saw, but when I looked for it, I couldn't find it.... I searched for it all over the house, but it was not there.... When I got to my office here on Fort Sam Houston, my electric saw was under my desk. I don't know to this day how that saw got under my desk."

16 The sergeant was sure no one could have borrowed or stolen his saw. He was equally certain he was not the one who put it in his office. "Such a thing worries you," he said at the time. "It is frightening."

17 *Frightening* was not the word most people used in describing Harvey, however. He never harmed anyone. Indeed, he seemed more playful than anything else. At Fort Sam Houston, people learned to take his antics in stride.

18 Harvey eventually left. Why, no one seems to know. Nothing has been heard from him in more than 15 years, and there are no indications that he will ever return. Service Club Number 2, now carrying the fashionable title of Hacienda Recreation Center, is once again a ghost-free gathering place.

19 Well then, who was Harvey, and what was he doing at the club? The most commonly accepted theory is that Harvey was the ghost of a young man who committed suicide in the club. But only the fact of the young man's violent death—not the *why* of it—is on record.

20 No matter who Harvey was and no matter why he decided to hang around Service Club Number 2, he provided some entertaining times for the folks at Fort Sam Houston.

If you have been timed while reading this article, enter your reading time below. Then turn to the Words-per-Minute Table on page 133 and look up your reading speed (words per minute). Enter your reading speed on the graph on page 134.

Reading Time: Lesson 14

_____ : _____
Minutes   Seconds

A Finding the Main Idea

One statement below expresses the main idea of the article. One statement is too general, or too broad. The other statement explains only part of the article; it is too narrow. Label the statements using the following key:

M—Main Idea **B—Too Broad** **N—Too Narrow**

_____ 1. Unexplained occurrences at Fort Sam Houston in Texas kept people there baffled for two years.

_____ 2. Though Harvey startled people and caused some problems, he never harmed anyone.

_____ 3. A playful ghost named Harvey baffled and entertained people at Service Club Number 2 at Fort Sam Houston in the late 1960s.

_____ Score 15 points for a correct M answer.

_____ Score 5 points for each correct B or N answer.

_____ **Total Score:** Finding the Main Idea

B Recalling Facts

How well do you remember the facts in the article? Put an X in the box next to the answer that correctly completes each statement about the article.

1. Service Club Number 2 was a
   ☐ a. sports club.
   ☐ b. recreation center.
   ☐ c. dining hall.

2. Phyllis Boyes's main problem with Harvey was that he
   ☐ a. played loud music at all hours.
   ☐ b. frightened people away from the club.
   ☐ c. kept opening the windows of the club.

3. One witness claimed to hear Harvey playing
   ☐ a. table tennis.
   ☐ b. pool.
   ☐ c. basketball.

4. The object that Sergeant Milligan said was missing from his home and then turned up in his office was
   ☐ a. an ax.
   ☐ b. a hammer.
   ☐ c. a saw.

5. The most commonly accepted explanation for Harvey is that he was the ghost of
   ☐ a. a soldier who was killed in a battle at the fort in the Civil War.
   ☐ b. a man who killed himself in the club.
   ☐ c. the first commander of Fort Sam Houston.

Score 5 points for each correct answer.

_____ **Total Score:** Recalling Facts

C | Making Inferences

When you combine your own experience and information from a text to draw a conclusion that is not directly stated in that text, you are making an inference. Below are five statements that may or may not be inferences based on information in the article. Label the statements using the following key:

C—Correct Inference   F—Faulty Inference

_____ 1. Phyllis Boyes was a harsh and unreasonable person to work for.

_____ 2. Since Harvey left, no music has been played in Service Club Number 2.

_____ 3. Some people enjoyed having Harvey around the club.

_____ 4. Harvey played each trick only once.

_____ 5. Phyllis Boyes took her responsibility to protect the service club seriously.

Score 5 points for each correct answer.

_____ **Total Score:** Making Inferences

D | Using Words Precisely

Each numbered sentence below contains an underlined word or phrase from the article. Following the sentence are three definitions. One definition is closest to the meaning of the underlined word. One definition is opposite or nearly opposite. Label those two definitions using the following key. Do not label the remaining definition.

C—Closest   O—Opposite or Nearly Opposite

1. Finally, a ghost seemed to be the only underlined plausible answer.

_____ a. improbable

_____ b. believable

_____ c. secret

2. Harvey was not malicious, as some ghosts are, but he could make quite a nuisance of himself.

_____ a. invisible

_____ b. vicious

_____ c. good-natured

3. So closing up the place and securing it is very important.

_____ a. locking

_____ b. watching

_____ c. freeing

4. The janitors, who were intimately familiar with all the nooks and crannies of the building, were asked to check every possible hiding place.

_____ a. closely

_____ b. unusually

_____ c. only slightly

5. Nothing has been heard from him in more than 15 years, and there are no <u>indications</u> that he will ever return.

_____ a. signs

_____ b. lack of evidence

_____ c. expectations

_____ Score 3 points for each correct C answer.

_____ Score 2 points for each correct O answer.

_____ **Total Score:** Using Words Precisely

Enter the four total scores in the spaces below, and add them together to find your Reading Comprehension Score. Then record your score on the graph on page 135.

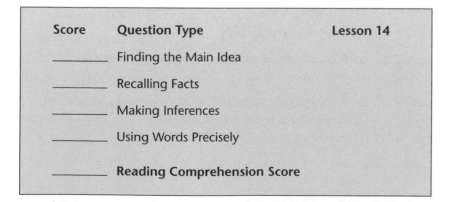

Score	Question Type	Lesson 14
_____	Finding the Main Idea	
_____	Recalling Facts	
_____	Making Inferences	
_____	Using Words Precisely	
_____	**Reading Comprehension Score**	

Author's Approach

Put an X in the box next to the correct answer.

1. The main purpose of the first paragraph is to

☐ a. describe the strange happenings at Service Club Number 2.

☐ b. convey a fearful mood.

☐ c. tell the reader when Harvey haunted Service Club Number 2.

2. In this article, "At Fort Sam Houston, people learned to take his antics in stride" means that people

☐ a. got used to Harvey's tricks.

☐ b. learned to avoid Harvey.

☐ c. ran away in fear when Harvey was around.

3. Choose the statement below that best explains how the author addresses the opposing point of view in the article.

☐ a. The author states that Harvey could occasionally be heard clearing his throat.

☐ b. The author states that Harvey is the ghost of a young man who committed suicide in the club.

☐ c. The author relates the experience of people who investigated some of the strange occurrences looking for an explanation that did not assume the existence of a ghost.

4. The author tells this story mainly by

☐ a. telling Sergeant Milligan's personal experiences with Harvey.

☐ b. telling different people's stories about Harvey.

☐ c. telling stories about different ghosts in Service Club Number 2.

_____ Number of correct answers

Record your personal assessment of your work on the Critical Thinking Chart on page 136.

CRITICAL THINKING

Summarizing and Paraphrasing

Put an X in the box next to the correct answer.

1. Below are summaries of the article. Choose the summary that says all the most important things about the article but in the fewest words.

   ☐ a. No one knows who Harvey was or why he haunted Service Club Number 2 at Fort Sam Houston, but for a few years in the late 1960s, Harvey was blamed for opening windows, playing music, and playing other harmless tricks.

   ☐ b. In the late 1960s, a ghost called Harvey played mischievous but harmless tricks on people in a club at Fort Sam Houston.

   ☐ c. For a few years, a ghost haunted a club at Fort Sam Houston.

2. Read the statement about the article below. Then read the paraphrase of that statement. Choose the reason that best tells why the paraphrase does not say the same thing as the statement.

   Statement: Eventually, Harvey was blamed for leaving windows open in the service club, but, in the beginning, Phyllis Boyes thought that the young men entrusted with securing the building were responsible.

   Paraphrase: The young men in charge of locking up the service club were not very responsible, and that's why Phyllis Boyes thought that Harvey opened the windows.

   ☐ a. Paraphrase says too much.

   ☐ b. Paraphrase doesn't say enough.

   ☐ c. Paraphrase doesn't agree with the statement about the article.

3. Choose the sentence that correctly restates the following sentence from the article:

   "There didn't seem to be any way that a person could have left the building without being noticed, either, unless, of course, that 'someone' happened to be a ghost!"

   ☐ a. No one could have left the building without being noticed.

   ☐ b. No one but a ghost could have left the building without being noticed.

   ☐ c. No one ever noticed when the ghost left the building.

   _____ Number of correct answers

   Record your personal assessment of your work on the Critical Thinking Chart on page 136.

Critical Thinking

Follow the directions provided for questions 1 and 3. Put an X in the box next to the correct answer for questions 2 and 4.

1. For each statement below, write O if it expresses an opinion and write F if it expresses a fact.

   _____ a. The Military Police at Fort Sam Houston take possible break-ins very seriously.

   _____ b. Most people would enjoy having a ghost like Harvey in their home.

   _____ c. Sergeant Milligan found his electric saw in his office but couldn't figure out how it got there.

2. Judging from Harvey's actions as told in this article, you can predict that he

☐ a. would attack anyone who didn't believe in him.

☐ b. would do anything to destroy the lives of the staff members of Fort Sam Houston.

☐ c. would never hurt anyone.

3. Read paragraph 9. Then choose from the letters below to correctly complete the following statement. Write the letters on the lines.

According to paragraph 9, _____ because _____.

a. the young soldier demanded that Harvey prove his existence

b. a door was wide open

c. a door slammed behind a young soldier

4. How is this article about Harvey related to stories about apparitions?

☐ a. The strange happenings at the service club strongly suggest the interference of a supernatural force.

☐ b. Harvey played harmless pranks.

☐ c. No one knows where Harvey got his name.

_____ Number of correct answers

Record your personal assessment of your work on the Critical Thinking Chart on page 136.

Personal Response

Why do you think Harvey haunted Service Club Number 2?

_____

_____

_____

_____

Self-Assessment

One of the things I did best when reading this article was

_____

_____

_____

I believe I did this well because

_____

_____

_____

_____

CRITICAL THINKING

Compare and Contrast

Think about the articles you have read in Unit Two. Pick the four articles that describe the apparitions who had the saddest stories. Write the titles in the first column of the chart below. Use information you learned from the articles to fill in the empty boxes in the chart.

Title	What details make this story particularly sad or tragic?	For what reasons does the apparition supposedly haunt the living?	What has been the reaction of the living to this apparition?

Choose the apparition you would most or least like to see. Explain why you chose him or her, and tell what you would say to that spirit if you ever met.

_____

_____

Words-per-Minute Table

Unit Two

Directions: If you were timed while reading an article, refer to the Reading Time you recorded in the box at the end of the article. Use this words-per-minute table to determine your reading speed for that article. Then plot your reading speed on the graph on page 134.

Lesson No. of Words	8 1131	9 1289	10 968	11 1173	12 1470	13 1085	14 1279	Seconds
1:30	754	859	645	782	980	723	853	90
1:40	679	773	581	704	882	651	767	100
1:50	617	703	528	640	802	592	698	110
2:00	566	645	484	587	735	543	640	120
2:10	522	595	447	541	678	501	590	130
2:20	485	552	415	503	630	465	548	140
2:30	452	516	387	469	588	434	512	150
2:40	424	483	363	440	551	407	480	160
2:50	399	455	342	414	519	383	451	170
3:00	377	430	323	391	490	362	426	180
3:10	357	407	306	370	464	343	404	190
3:20	339	387	290	352	441	326	384	200
3:30	323	368	277	335	420	310	365	210
3:40	308	352	264	320	401	296	349	220
3:50	295	336	253	306	383	283	334	230
4:00	283	322	242	293	368	271	320	240
4:10	271	309	232	282	353	260	307	250
4:20	261	297	223	271	339	250	295	260
4:30	251	286	215	261	327	241	284	270
4:40	242	276	207	251	315	233	274	280
4:50	234	267	200	243	304	224	265	290
5:00	226	258	194	235	294	217	256	300
5:10	219	249	187	227	285	210	248	310
5:20	212	242	182	220	276	203	240	320
5:30	206	234	176	213	267	197	233	330
5:40	200	227	171	207	259	191	226	340
5:50	194	221	166	201	252	186	219	350
6:00	189	215	161	196	245	181	213	360
6:10	183	209	157	190	238	176	207	370
6:20	179	204	153	185	232	171	202	380
6:30	174	198	149	180	226	167	197	390
6:40	170	193	145	176	221	163	192	400
6:50	166	189	142	172	215	159	187	410
7:00	162	184	138	168	210	155	183	420
7:10	158	180	135	164	205	151	179	430
7:20	154	176	132	160	200	148	174	440
7:30	151	172	129	156	196	145	171	450
7:40	148	168	126	153	192	142	167	460
7:50	144	165	124	150	188	139	163	470
8:00	141	161	121	147	184	136	160	480

Minutes and Seconds

Plotting Your Progress: Reading Speed

Unit Two

Directions: If you were timed while reading an article, write your words-per-minute rate for that article in the box under the number of the lesson. Then plot your reading speed on the graph by putting a small X on the line directly above the number of the lesson, across from the number of words per minute you read. As you mark your speed for each lesson, graph your progress by drawing a line to connect the X's.

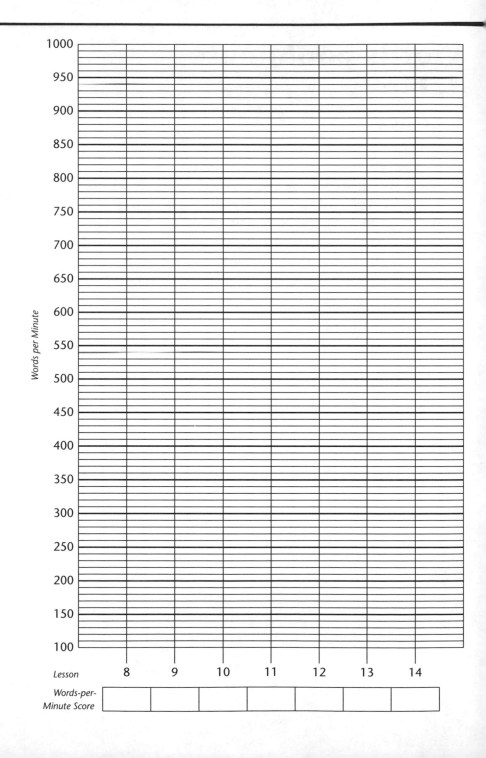

Plotting Your Progress: Reading Comprehension

Unit Two

Directions: Write your Reading Comprehension score for each lesson in the box under the number of the lesson. Then plot your score on the graph by putting a small X on the line directly above the number of the lesson and across from the score you earned. As you mark your score for each lesson, graph your progress by drawing a line to connect the X's.

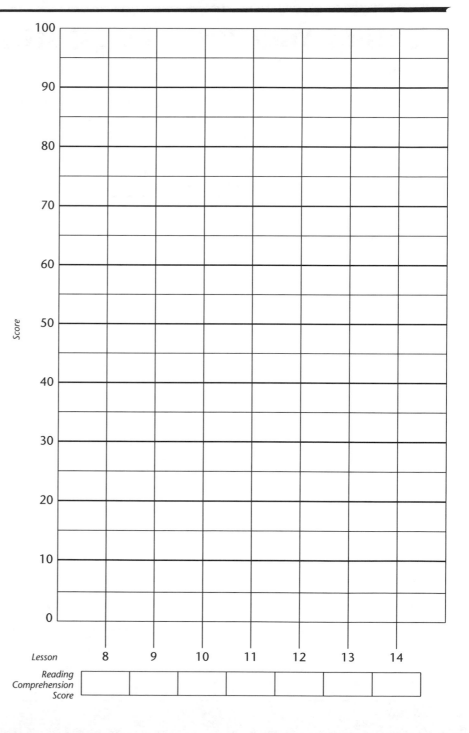

Lesson	8	9	10	11	12	13	14
Reading Comprehension Score							

Plotting Your Progress: Critical Thinking

Unit Two

Directions: Work with your teacher to evaluate your responses to the Critical Thinking questions for each lesson. Then fill in the appropriate spaces in the chart below. For each lesson and each type of Critical Thinking question, do the following: Mark a minus sign (–) in the box to indicate areas in which you feel you could improve. Mark a plus sign (+) to indicate areas in which you feel you did well. Mark a minus-slash-plus sign (–/+) to indicate areas in which you had mixed success. Then write any comments you have about your performance, including ideas for improvement.

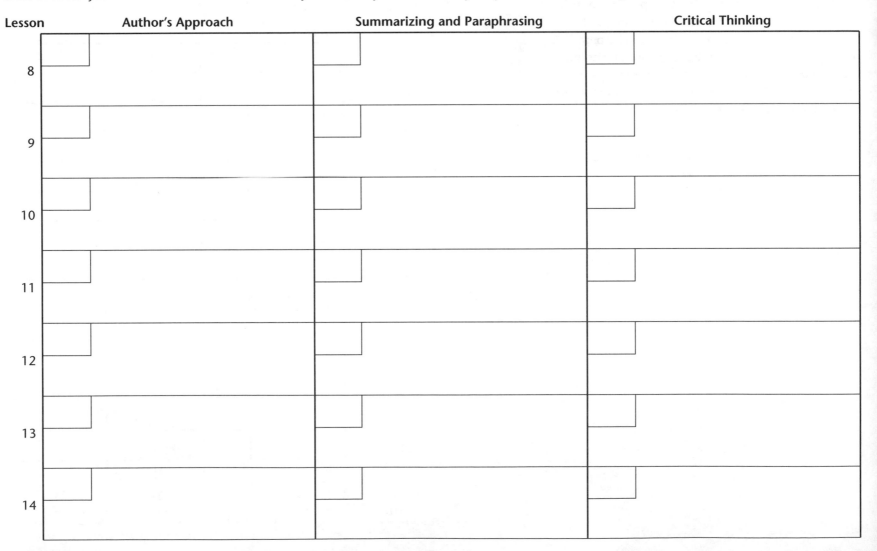

Lesson	Author's Approach	Summarizing and Paraphrasing	Critical Thinking
8			
9			
10			
11			
12			
13			
14			

UNIT THREE

THE RETURN OF NELLY BUTLER

Nelly Butler is buried in this church cemetery in Machiasport, Maine.

One day late in January, in the year 1800, Captain Paul Blaisdel saw a most unusual sight. He was walking through a field when an "unreal-looking" figure of a woman appeared in the distance. Her clothes, he later said, were "as white as possible," and she seemed to float over the ground. The apparition moved quickly toward him, but before Blaisdel could say a word, it vanished into thin air.

2   Ghosts were not common in the town of Machiasport, Maine. Until then, there was no record of anyone in the town ever having seen one. But Paul Blaisdel's ghostly encounter was only the beginning of what would prove to be a unique supernatural experience for scores of people in that seacoast town.

3   Paul Blaisdel was the first to see the apparition, but a few months earlier, on August 9, 1799, the spirit had made its presence known at the home of Paul's father, Abner Blaisdel. A voice, seeming to come out of nowhere, announced to the family that its ghostly figure would soon appear in the village. The Blaisdels were dumbfounded. They had no idea whom the voice belonged to. But they did know

enough to keep the story to themselves, since the hard-working, practical people of Machiasport would certainly have laughed in their faces.

4   As months went by and the voice remained silent, the Blaisdels forgot about the announcement. On January 2, 1800, however, the voice spoke again. That time it revealed its owner. "I am Captain George Butler's deceased wife, Nelly," it said. "My father is David Hooper."

5   The Blaisdels knew both these men well. In fact, they had also known Nelly Butler before her death. "Send two messengers to fetch my father," the voice ordered in a tone that left no room for argument. The Blaisdels did as they were told.

6   David Hooper was an old man, and six miles was a long trip for what he considered "plumb foolishness," but when he got to the Blaisdel house and heard the voice, he was convinced that it was indeed his daughter speaking. Later he wrote that she gave "such clear and irresistible tokens of her being the spirit of my own daughter as gave me no less satisfaction than admiration and delight."

7   Later that month, "the spectre," as the townsfolk called the apparition, appeared to Paul Blaisdel in the field. Apparently, though, she was not happy with his reaction. The day after the encounter, Nelly appeared at the Blaisdel home to chide Paul for being rude to an old friend and neighbor.

8   After that visit, Nelly stayed away for several weeks. She returned again in March for a chat. She insisted that all four Blaisdels gather in the cellar, where she talked to them for two hours. "Though my body is consumed and turned to dust," she said, "my soul is as much alive as before I left the body."

9   In May she returned six nights in a row. By that time the apparition was the talk of the town, and the Blaisdels were being bombarded with visitors. The curious were taken to the cellar, which was the spectre's favorite spot. According to witnesses, the spectre usually appeared dressed in shining white, and the brightness of her body lit the area around her. All agreed that she looked like the person she said she was—the deceased Nelly Butler.

10   One witness, Mary Gordon, who visited the Blaisdels' cellar as part of a group, described her experience with the spectre this way: "At first the apparition was a mere mass of light. Then it grew into personal form, about as tall as myself. We stood in two ranks, about four or five feet apart. Between these ranks she slowly passed and repassed, so that any of us could have handled her. When she passed by me, her nearness was that of contact, so that if there had been a substance, I should have certainly felt it. The glow of the apparition had a constant tremulous motion. At last the personal form became shapeless—expanded every way, and then vanished in a moment."

11   Despite the written testimony of dozens of witnesses, many people were skeptical of the apparition. One doubter was Abraham Cummings, a minister and a well-educated man. But Cummings changed his mind when he saw the spectre for himself. Crossing an open field

The town of Machiasport nestles along the northern coast of Maine.

in front of his house, the minister saw a group of white rocks on a small hill about two hundred feet in front of him. As he walked toward them, one of the rocks rose off the ground and began taking the shape of a globe of rosy light. Suddenly the light moved near to him, and took on the shape of a very tiny woman. She grew to normal size, and Cummings said she looked "glorious," with rays of light shining from her head like a halo reaching to the ground.

12   That experience changed the minister's life. He became a convert, and set out to record every appearance the spectre made. He later published an account of the events, which included the testimony of every witness he could contact. Several copies of Abraham Cummings's pamphlet are still in existence (one of them can be found in the Brown University library, in Rhode Island), but Cummings was, unfortunately, a boring and often confusing writer.

13   Though Cummings grew to believe in the existence of the spectre, there were many who suspected the Blaisdels of fraud. One reason for their suspicion was the fact that the spectre ordered her former husband, Captain George Butler, to marry Abner Blaisdel's daughter Lydia. Abner said he was against the marriage, and so did Lydia. Although she was attracted to George, she refused to "marry a man who has been scared into proposing by a ghost."

14   However, when Captain Butler insisted that he wanted to marry Lydia for himself, and not because his dead wife ordered him to, Lydia changed her mind. Then the gossiping began in earnest. Folks said that Lydia had thought up the hoax to get herself a husband.

15   The spectre tried to prove Lydia's innocence. Once she appeared to a large gathering at which Lydia was present. She ordered Lydia to go to another room, where she was watched by two women. While Lydia was gone, Nelly continued to carry on in the cellar, proving that Lydia had no part in her performance. Another time the spectre marched next to Lydia in a funeral procession, so that everyone could see the two of them together.

16   Nonetheless, the gossip and suspicions continued. Finally, unable to bear up against the accusations, Lydia broke her engagement and made plans to visit relatives who lived farther down the coast. But before she could sail away, the spectre intervened and convinced her that she could not escape the gossip. Lydia and George were married shortly afterward.

17   By that time, Nelly had been appearing in Machiasport for over a year. She seemed to enjoy showing off her powers, which included predicting the future. She told the Blaisdels of a lawsuit that they would be involved in, and of how it would come out. She also predicted some bad news. Shortly after Lydia and George were married, the spectre appeared to George. "Be kind to Lydia," she said, "for she will not be with you long. She will have one child and die within the year." Ten months after the wedding, Lydia gave birth and died the next day.

18   Captain Butler never doubted that the spectre was the spirit of his dead wife.

Nelly visited him several times and recalled conversations that they'd had during their life together—conversations that only she could have known about. Once she appeared before him carrying a very small child, a reminder, he thought, of the fact that she too had died in childbirth. Speaking of the apparition of the baby, Butler later said, "I reached out my left hand to take hold of it. I saw my hand in the middle of it, but could feel nothing." Four witnesses confirmed Butler's claim.

19   After Lydia's death, the spectre disappeared from Machiasport, never to return. Although more than 100 observers claimed to have seen or heard her, one important question remained unanswered: Why had she come in the first place?

20   Whatever the reason, Nelly Butler holds a special place in United States history. Thanks to Abraham Cummings, she was the first ghost to be written about in an account featuring sworn testimonies. And she was witnessed by more people than any other ghost, before or since. 🍂

If you have been timed while reading this article, enter your reading time below. Then turn to the Words-per-Minute Table on page 195 and look up your reading speed (words per minute). Enter your reading speed on the graph on page 196.

Reading Time: **Lesson 14**

_____ : _____
Minutes   Seconds

Finding the Main Idea

One statement below expresses the main idea of the article. One statement is too general, or too broad. The other statement explains only part of the article; it is too narrow. Label the statements using the following key:

M—Main Idea   **B—Too Broad**   **N—Too Narrow**

_____ 1. The ghost of Nelly Butler appeared in Machiasport, Maine, many times around 1800, becoming the most widely witnessed ghost in history.

_____ 2. Nelly Butler's ghost appeared in Machiasport, Maine.

_____ 3. A ghost in a small New England town captured the attention of the townspeople for more than a year in the early 19th century.

_____ Score 15 points for a correct M answer.

_____ Score 5 points for each correct B or N answer.

_____ **Total Score:** Finding the Main Idea

B **Recalling Facts**

How well do you remember the facts in the article? Put an X in the box next to the answer that correctly completes each statement about the article.

1. The first person the ghost of Nelly Butler appeared to was
☐ a. Paul Blaisdel.
☐ b. George Butler.
☐ c. Abner Blaisdel.

2. Nelly's favorite place to meet with people was in a
☐ a. field.
☐ b. cemetery.
☐ c. cellar.

3. The main thing people noticed about the ghost of Nelly Butler was
☐ a. the softness of her voice.
☐ b. brightness and light.
☐ c. her sense of humor.

4. Lydia Blaisdel was going to leave Machiasport because she
☐ a. didn't want to marry George Butler.
☐ b. was afraid of the ghost of Nelly Butler.
☐ c. couldn't stand the unkind gossip people were spreading about her.

5. The ghost of Nelly Butler left Machiasport when
☐ a. Lydia Blaisdel died.
☐ b. George Butler remarried.
☐ c. Abraham Cummings had finished his book.

Score 5 points for each correct answer.

_____ **Total Score:** Recalling Facts

C | Making Inferences

When you combine your own experience and information from a text to draw a conclusion that is not directly stated in that text, you are making an inference. Below are five statements that may or may not be inferences based on information in the article. Label the statements using the following key:

C—Correct Inference   **F—Faulty Inference**

_____ 1. Most people in Machiasport were afraid of the ghost of Nelly Butler.

_____ 2. Lydia's baby died at the same time as Lydia died.

_____ 3. David Hooper was happy to talk to the ghost of his daughter.

_____ 4. Nelly Butler liked Lydia Blaisdel.

_____ 5. George Butler never married again after Lydia's death.

Score 5 points for each correct answer.

_____ **Total Score:** Making Inferences

D | Using Words Precisely

Each numbered sentence below contains an underlined word or phrase from the article. Following the sentence are three definitions. One definition is closest to the meaning of the underlined word. One definition is opposite or nearly opposite. Label those two definitions using the following key. Do not label the remaining definition.

C—Closest   **O—Opposite or Nearly Opposite**

1. The Blaisdels were <u>dumbfounded</u>.

_____ a. stupid

_____ b. uninterested and bored

_____ c. astonished and confused

2. "Send two messengers to <u>fetch</u> my father," the voice ordered in a tone that left no room for argument.

_____ a. get

_____ b. rescue

_____ c. leave

3. The day after the encounter, Nelly appeared at the Blaisdel home to <u>chide</u> Paul for being rude to an old friend and neighbor.

_____ a. remind

_____ b. praise

_____ c. scold

4. Despite the written testimony of dozens of witnesses, many people were <u>skeptical</u> of the apparition.

_____ a. sure

_____ b. doubtful

_____ c. terrified

5. But before she could sail away, the spectre <u>intervened</u> and convinced her that she could not escape the gossip.

_____ a. interfered

_____ b. withdrew

_____ c. floated away

_____ Score 3 points for each correct C answer.

_____ Score 2 points for each correct O answer.

_____ **Total Score:** Using Words Precisely

Enter the four total scores in the spaces below, and add them together to find your Reading Comprehension Score. Then record your score on the graph on page 197.

Score	Question Type	Lesson 15
_____	Finding the Main Idea	
_____	Recalling Facts	
_____	Making Inferences	
_____	Using Words Precisely	
_____	**Reading Comprehension Score**	

Author's Approach

Put an X in the box next to the correct answer.

1. What does the author mean by the statement "'Send two messengers to fetch my father,' the voice ordered in a tone that left no room for argument"?

☐ a. The voice refused to listen to their arguments.

☐ b. The voice filled the room with sound.

☐ c. The voice used a very demanding tone.

2. The main purpose of the first paragraph is to

☐ a. convey a mood of terror.

☐ b. describe the first sighting of Nelly Butler's ghost.

☐ c. explain Captain Paul Blaisdel's relationship to Nelly Butler.

3. What does the author imply by saying "But they did know enough to keep the story to themselves, since the hard-working, practical people of Machiasport would certainly have laughed in their faces"?

☐ a. Most of the people in Machiasport had a good sense of humor.

☐ b. The Blaisdels didn't want to share their ghost with anyone.

☐ c. The people of Machiasport wouldn't have believed the Blaisdels.

4. The author tells this story mainly by

☐ a. retelling personal experiences.

☐ b. telling different stories about the same topic.

☐ c. using his or her imagination and creativity.

_____ Number of correct answers

Record your personal assessment of your work on the Critical Thinking Chart on page 198.

CRITICAL THINKING

Summarizing and Paraphrasing

Follow the directions provided for questions 1 and 2. Put an X in the box next to the correct answer for question 3.

1. Complete the following one-sentence summary of the article using the lettered phrases from the phrase bank below. Write the letters on the lines.

> **Phrase Bank:**
> a. Nelly's appearance before the Blaisdel family
> b. Nelly's final disappearance
> c. the reactions and descriptions of other witnesses who saw Nelly

After describing the appearance of Nelly Butler's ghost to Paul Blaisdel, the article discusses _____, goes on to explain _____, and ends with _____.

2. Reread paragraph 11 in the article. Below, write a summary of the paragraph in no more than 25 words.

_____

_____

_____

_____

Reread your summary and decide whether it covers the important ideas in the paragraph. Next, decide how to shorten the summary to 15 words or less without leaving out any essential information. Write this summary below.

_____

_____

3. Choose the best one-sentence paraphrase for the following sentence from the article:

"Later [David Hooper] wrote that she gave 'such clear and irresistible tokens of her being the spirit of my own daughter as gave me no less satisfaction than admiration and delight.'"

☐ a. David Hooper wrote that he was satisfied and delighted that the spirit was that of his daughter.

☐ b. David Hooper wrote that he had always admired and been delighted by his daughter.

☐ c. David Hooper wrote that he was very pleased with the gifts Nelly gave him.

> _____ Number of correct answers
>
> Record your personal assessment of your work on the Critical Thinking Chart on page 198.

Critical Thinking

Put an X in the box next to the correct answer for question 1. Follow the directions provided for the other questions.

1. From what Captain George Butler said, you can predict that if Nelly hadn't ordered him to marry Lydia, he

☐ a. would have preferred it if someone else had married Lydia.

☐ b. never would have had the courage to ask for Lydia's hand in marriage.

☐ c. would have asked Lydia to marry him anyway.

2. Choose from the letters below to correctly complete the following statement. Write the letters on the lines.

   In the article, _____ and _____ are alike.

   a. Lydia Blaisdel's experience with childbirth

   b. Mary Gordon's experience with childbirth

   c. Nelly Butler's experience with childbirth

3. Choose from the letters below to correctly complete the following statement. Write the letters on the lines.

   According to the article, _____ caused Abraham Cummings to _____, and the effect was _____.

   a. believe that Nelly's apparition was real

   b. the eerie appearance of a ghostly woman

   c. he tried to record every appearance the spectre made

4. Which paragraphs from the article provide evidence that supports your answer to question 2?

_____

_____ Number of correct answers

Record your personal assessment of your work on the Critical Thinking Chart on page 198.

Personal Response

This article is different from other articles about apparitions I've read because

_____

_____

_____

and Nelly Butler is unlike other spirits because

_____

_____

_____

_____

Self-Assessment

Which concepts or ideas from the article were difficult to understand?

_____

_____

_____

Which were easy to understand?

_____

_____

_____

_____

A BEVERLY HILLS GHOST
Haunting the Rich and Famous

Actress Elke Sommer stands amid some of the charred ruins of her haunted Beverly Hills home.

The residents of Beverly Hills, California, include some of the most famous faces in the world—movie stars, sports figures, TV personalities. At least one of the residents of that well-known city has had an uninvited and decidedly unwelcome housemate—one that caused a lot of confusion and not a little consternation.

2   Actress Elke Sommer and her husband, reporter Joe Hyams, met the intruder shortly after moving into their new house in July of 1964. A guest of theirs, a journalist named Edith Dohlfield, was having tea by the pool when she noticed a man suddenly appear, walk quickly around the pool, and then disappear. She later described the man as middle-aged, husky, and broad-shouldered, with a "potato nose." He was wearing dark slacks with a white shirt and a tie. When Edith asked who the man was, Elke and Joe said they had no idea.

3   A similar experience was reported about two weeks later. A person cleaning the pool said he saw an older, heavy-set man with graying hair walking quickly toward the dining room. The stranger was

dressed in dark trousers and a white shirt with a tie. Since the pool cleaner had been told that the owners were away and the house would be empty, he decided to investigate. When he followed the man into the house, however, he found no trace of anyone.

4   Elke Sommer's mother, who was visiting at the house, was the third person to see the strange man. He woke her in the middle of the night. Just as she was about to scream, he vanished into thin air.

5   Up to that point, neither Elke Sommer nor Joe Hyams had noticed anything out of the ordinary in their new house. Then they began hearing strange noises, such as the sound of chairs scraping across the floor in the dining room at night. Whenever they checked the room, however, everything was in its proper place.

6   In August, when Elke was making a film in Yugoslavia and Joe was staying alone in the house, he witnessed a series of unexplainable events. Each morning he found a bedroom window on the first floor wide open, even though he always locked the window at night. At times he heard the front door open and shut when no one else was in the house. Although he was growing more and more concerned about the strange things that were happening, Hyams was sure there was a logical explanation for everything.

A journalist for 15 years, he was a believer in facts.

7   Determined to get to the bottom of the matter, he bought three small radio transmitters and set them up in different places: at the end of the driveway, at the front door, and in the dining room. He wired three tape recorders to the transmitters and hooked them up, in turn, to three fm radios, which he placed upstairs in his bedroom. When the equipment was turned on, any sounds made near the transmitters would be heard in the bedroom and would also be recorded. Using chalk, Joe then marked the placement of each dining room chair so that he could tell if any of the chairs had been moved.

8   His efforts were soon rewarded. On the first night of his surveillance, he heard the same scraping sounds he had heard so often before. He stole quietly down the stairs and into the dining room, only to find that no one was there and the chairs were all in their proper places. As soon as he went back upstairs, though, the noises resumed.

9   In September John Sherlock, a writer friend whom Joe Hyams described as having a "cool, careful mind," stayed in the house while Elke and Joe were away. He heard the same noises and noticed the same strange and inexplicable opening of

the downstairs window. When he was preparing to go to bed one evening, he suddenly had the eerie sensation that someone was watching him. He turned to see a man staring at him from the doorway—a man wearing dark trousers, a white shirt, and a dark tie. Sherlock was so frightened that he immediately moved into a motel. "I never had such a feeling of menace," he later told Hyams.

10   The same strange events persisted, and new ones were added. A detective who

Elke Sommer and her husband Joe Hyams at the Academy Awards in 1965

had been hired to watch the house reported that once all the lights in the house were turned on at the same time; there was no one home. Also Elke and Joe's two dogs started acting restless and standing at the entrance to the dining room, barking at nothing. The strange noises continued.

11 Still sure that there had to be a logical explanation, Hyams hired a team of termite inspectors to look for hidden entrances to the house. None were found. An architect hired to search for hidden rooms in the house also found nothing.

12 Finally, at Joe Hyams's request, professional ghost hunters became involved in the case. They began by questioning the four witnesses who had reported seeing the strange man. Each was asked to describe the man, including what he looked like, what he had been doing when they saw him, and what kind of impression he gave. The witnesses were asked to be as specific as possible. One of the investigative team, who remained in New York, then analyzed the reports in an attempt to come up with a composite description of the man.

13 The next step was to bring a number of strangers into the house, one at a time, to see if they could sense a presence. Some of the people selected said that they had never seen a ghost before. Others were "sensitives"—people who claim to be able to communicate with spirits. Although no one had been told any details about the apparition in Elke and Joe's house, four of the people said that they sensed a

presence in the dining room, and three described a man who sounded much like the one seen by the four witnesses. Some of the details of the man's appearance reminded Joe Hyams of a doctor he had worked with who had recently died. He also sounded somewhat like Elke Sommer's father, who was dead.

14 The sensitives provided further impressions. One claimed to have seen a girl near the pool, and gave a description that sounded much like a girl whom Elke Sommer had known in Europe and who had died recently. Another sensitive predicted that there would be a fire in the house, perhaps within six months, and that it would be raining at the time. She also predicted that Elke and Joe would move out of the house within two years.

15 The conclusion drawn by the ghost hunters was somewhat disappointing. It was possible, but only possible, they said, that the house was haunted. Without more evidence, they were unwilling to make a more definite statement.

16 By that time, however, Elke and Joe had reached their own conclusion. Thorough searches of the house by termite inspectors, private detectives, and electronics experts had convinced them that no human being or animal was causing the problems. A geologist had reported that the land was not shifting. A construction expert had stated that the house was solid. After eliminating every logical explanation, Joe Hyams stated, "Even I am reluctantly convinced that we have at least one ghost in the house. But,"

he added, "we don't intend to move out. I would not let a living man frighten me out of my house, and I certainly don't intend to let a dead one do it."

17 It wasn't long before he changed his mind. Early in the morning, on March 13, 1967, during a rare California rainstorm, Elke and Joe were awakened by loud pounding on their bedroom door. When they opened the door, they were engulfed by smoke. The house was on fire. Luckily, they were able to crawl out a window to safety, and fire fighters arrived in time to put out the blaze.

18 Although an investigation into the fire was unable to pinpoint a cause, it was found that the fire had started in the dining room. Enough was enough, Elke and Joe decided. Just as the sensitive had predicted, they moved to a new house—one that contained no uninvited guests.

If you have been timed while reading this article, enter your reading time below. Then turn to the Words-per-Minute Table on page 195 and look up your reading speed (words per minute). Enter your reading speed on the graph on page 196.

Reading Time: Lesson 16

_____ : _____
Minutes   Seconds

A | Finding the Main Idea

One statement below expresses the main idea of the article. One statement is too general, or too broad. The other statement explains only part of the article; it is too narrow. Label the statements using the following key:

M—Main Idea **B—Too Broad** **N—Too Narrow**

_____ 1. Elke Sommer and Joe Hyams were forced to leave their house by an intruder that they finally decided had to be a ghost.

_____ 2. Strange occurrences in Elke Sommer and Joe Hyams's house frightened and perplexed those who stayed in the house.

_____ 3. In and just outside Elke Sommer and Joe Hyams's house, a number of people saw a strange man appear and then vanish.

_____ Score 15 points for a correct M answer.

_____ Score 5 points for each correct B or N answer.

_____ **Total Score:** Finding the Main Idea

B | Recalling Facts

How well do you remember the facts in the article? Put an X in the box next to the answer that correctly completes each statement about the article.

1. Joe Hyams was a
   ☐ a. movie director.
   ☐ b. journalist.
   ☐ c. record producer.

2. The strange man was first seen
   ☐ a. near the pool.
   ☐ b. entering the dining room.
   ☐ c. near the bedroom door.

3. The ghost hunters concluded that
   ☐ a. the house was definitely haunted.
   ☐ b. there was no ghost in the house.
   ☐ c. it was possible that the house was haunted.

4. The fire in the house
   ☐ a. originated in the bedroom.
   ☐ b. took place during a rainstorm.
   ☐ c. destroyed most of the house.

5. Elke and Joe became convinced that
   ☐ a. there was a ghost in the house.
   ☐ b. someone was playing an unpleasant hoax on them.
   ☐ c. someone who didn't like them was trying to frighten them.

Score 5 points for each correct answer.

_____ **Total Score:** Recalling Facts

C | Making Inferences

When you combine your own experience and information from a text to draw a conclusion that is not directly stated in that text, you are making an inference. Below are five statements that may or may not be inferences based on information in the article. Label the statements using the following key:

C—Correct Inference   F—Faulty Inference

_____ 1. No one ever found out who the strange man was.

_____ 2. The strange man never spoke.

_____ 3. The ghost hunters were frauds.

_____ 4. Neither Elke nor Joe ever became frightened of the presence in their house.

_____ 5. No one has lived in the house since Elke and Joe moved out.

Score 5 points for each correct answer.

_____ **Total Score:** Making Inferences

D | Using Words Precisely

Each numbered sentence below contains an underlined word or phrase from the article. Following the sentence are three definitions. One definition is closest to the meaning of the underlined word. One definition is opposite or nearly opposite. Label those two definitions using the following key. Do not label the remaining definition.

C—Closest   O—Opposite or Nearly Opposite

1. At least one of the residents of that well-known city has had an uninvited and decidedly unwelcome housemate—one that caused a lot of confusion and not a little <u>consternation</u>.

   _____ a. comfort

   _____ b. alarm

   _____ c. misunderstanding

2. On the first night of his <u>surveillance</u>, he heard the same scraping sounds he had heard so often before.

   _____ a. vacation

   _____ b. ignoring

   _____ c. supervision

3. He <u>stole</u> quietly down the stairs and into the dining room, only to find that no one was there and the chairs were all in their proper places.

   _____ a. fell

   _____ b. moved boldly

   _____ c. sneaked

4. He heard the same noises and noticed the same strange and <u>inexplicable</u> opening of the downstairs window.

_____ a. unexplainable

_____ b. enjoyable

_____ c. understandable

5. "I never had such a feeling of <u>menace</u>," he later told Hyams.

_____ a. embarrassment

_____ b. safety

_____ c. threat

_____ Score 3 points for each correct C answer.

_____ Score 2 points for each correct O answer.

_____ **Total Score:** Using Words Precisely

Enter the four total scores in the spaces below, and add them together to find your Reading Comprehension Score. Then record your score on the graph on page 197.

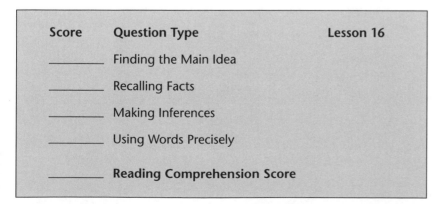

Score	Question Type	Lesson 16
_____	Finding the Main Idea	
_____	Recalling Facts	
_____	Making Inferences	
_____	Using Words Precisely	
_____	**Reading Comprehension Score**	

Author's Approach

Put an X in the box next to the correct answer.

1. What is the author's purpose in writing "A Beverly Hills Ghost"?

☐ a. To persuade the reader that Elke Sommer's house was haunted

☐ b. To inform the reader about the steps Elke and Joe took to investigate the unexplainable events in their home

☐ c. To convey an angry mood

2. From the statement "…John Sherlock, a writer friend…described as having a 'cool, careful mind,' stayed in the house…" you can conclude that the author wants the reader to think that Sherlock

☐ a. had had a lot of experience with ghosts.

☐ b. was a cold, unfeeling man.

☐ c. was reasonable and calm.

3. How is the author's purpose for writing the article expressed in paragraph 16? (OK to look)

☐ a. The author describes Joe's growing feeling of terror as he realizes that at least one ghost is living in his house.

☐ b. The author cites evidence proving that the house was haunted.

☐ c. The author tells how Elke and Joe eliminated every logical explanation for the strange sights and sounds in their house.

4. The author tells this story mainly by

☐ a. retelling Elke and Joe's personal experiences.

☐ b. comparing different movie stars' experiences with ghosts.

☐ c. revealing the opinions of sensitives.

_____ Number of correct answers

Record your personal assessment of your work on the Critical Thinking Chart on page 198.

CRITICAL THINKING

Summarizing and Paraphrasing

Follow the directions provided for the questions 1 and 2. Put an X in the box next to the correct answer for question 3.

1. Complete the following one-sentence summary of the article using the lettered phrases from the phrase bank below. Write the letters on the lines.

> **Phrase Bank:**
> a. sightings of a strange man in Elke and Joe's house
> b. Joe's efforts to find a logical explanation for the odd events in his home
> c. Elke and Joe's decision to move away after their house catches fire

The article about the Beverly Hills ghost begins with _____, goes on to explain _____, and ends with _____.

2. Reread paragraph 6 in the article. Below, write a summary of the paragraph in no more than 25 words.

_____

_____

_____

_____

Reread your summary and decide whether it covers the important ideas in the paragraph. Next, decide how to shorten the summary to 15 words or less without leaving out any essential information. Write this summary below.

_____

_____

_____

3. Choose the best one-sentence paraphrase for the following sentence from the article:

"Although no one had been told any details about the apparition in Elke and Joe's house, four of the people said that they sensed a presence in the dining room, and three described a man who sounded much like the one seen by the four witnesses."

☐ a. None of the people had been told much about the ghost, but four felt a presence in the dining room and three described someone who looked like the man seen by the four witnesses.

☐ b. Four people saw ghosts in the dining room, while three described a man who liked like the other four.

☐ c. Although no one had been told about the ghost in Elke and Joe's house, four witnesses described a man whose presence they sensed in the dining room.

_____ Number of correct answers

Record your personal assessment of your work on the Critical Thinking Chart on page 198.

CRITICAL THINKING

Critical Thinking

Put an X in the box next to the correct answer for questions 1 and 3. Follow the directions provided for questions 2 and 4.

1. From what Joe Hyams said, you can conclude that he

   ☐ a. hates to move.

   ☐ b. is scared to death of ghosts.

   ☐ c. is not easily frightened.

2. Choose from the letters below to correctly complete the following statement. Write the letters on the lines.

   In the article, _____ and _____ are alike.

   a. the apparition Edith Dohlfield saw

   b. the apparition seen by the sensitive who described a girl

   c. the apparition the pool cleaner saw

3. What was the effect of the fire in Elke and Joe's house?

   ☐ a. A sensitive predicted there would be a fire.

   ☐ b. They moved out.

   ☐ c. The fire had started in the dining room.

4. Which paragraphs from the article provide evidence that supports your answer to question 3?

   _____

_____ Number of correct answers

Record your personal assessment of your work on the Critical Thinking Chart on page 198.

Personal Response

I wonder why

_____

_____

_____

_____

Self-Assessment

While reading the article, I found it easiest to

_____

_____

_____

_____

THE HAUNTED U-BOAT

The German U-boat, Deutschland *(above), was captured during World War I. U-65 was a U-boat like the* Deutschland.

It was 1916, the midpoint of World War I, and the tide was beginning to turn against the Germans. Their soldiers were dug into positions in France, unable to advance. A British blockade of German harbors kept German supply ships from moving in and out of their own ports. In the United States, preparations to enter the war were underway; the country did so a year later. So it was no surprise when the Germans began building ships in the city of Bruges, Belgium, which they had occupied. The ships were *unterseeboots*, or U-boats, as German submarines were commonly called, and 24 of them were being built.

2   Construction went smoothly on the first 23 boats, but the 24th, designated the U-65, was another story. Several workers were killed while building it. Then on launching day, in October of 1916, as the U-65 was finally eased into the water, one of its officers fell overboard to his death.

3   That was far from the end of the submarine's troubles. U-65 put out to sea for trials, and on its first dive was stuck underwater, unable to resurface, for more than 12 hours. Sailors being a superstitious lot by nature, the crew was terrified at that near catastrophe. U-65 proceeded back to port, where it was examined thoroughly. No reason for the malfunction could be found.

4   The day after the examination, a torpedo exploded on deck during a loading exercise, killing an officer and five crewmen. That incident led to the first sighting of a ghost on board the U-65—the ghost of the officer killed in the torpedo explosion.

5   By that time, the story of the unlucky U-65 had made its way through the entire U-boat fleet. Sailors were convinced that the U-65 was a Jonah—a jinxed boat—and that it was haunted. More than one crewman reported seeing the ghost of the dead officer. "We saw him come aboard and walk slowly to the bow," one sailor insisted. "He stood there, staring at us, with his arms folded across his chest."

6   Stories of that sort can quickly demoralize the crew of any warship. That was something the German high command could not afford to let happen to the U-65. The enormously successful U-boats were Germany's chief weapon in the war. The country needed every one it could build.

7   Doing his part to restore morale, the captain of the U-65 mustered his crew on the afterdeck. He spoke of Germany's need for U-boats. He acknowledged the great strain everyone was under. Then he broached the subject of the ghost. "I'm sure it's just imagination," he said. "The accident was a sad experience for all of us. Just try to put it out of your minds."

8   Shortly after the captain's talk, the U-65 put out to sea on its first war patrol. That is when the ghost materialized on board for the second time. Even the captain was a witness. When the patrol ended, the U-65 headed back to Bruges, where it was to undergo normal maintenance before its next cruise against the enemy.

9   Back in port, another tragic incident occurred. Allied bombers struck Bruges in a lightning-fast raid, killing, among hundreds of others, the captain of the U-65. As might be expected, the talk of its being a Jonah revived.

10   This time Admiral Schroeder, head of the U-boat command, took matters into his own hands. After denouncing all talk of jinxed boats and ghosts as "superstitious nonsense," the admiral spent a night on board the U-65. In the morning he informed the crew that he had spent a restful night, undisturbed by any ghost. Still, to further placate the crew, he ordered that a clergyman perform an exorcism—a religious ceremony in which evil spirits are driven away—on board the U-65.

11   Admiral Schroeder's next step was to pick a new captain for the boat. He purposely chose a strict disciplinarian—Lieutenant Commander Gustav Schelle. The new captain immediately warned his crew that anyone even mentioning ghosts would be dealt with severely.

12   For nearly a year, through many war patrols, the U-65 performed admirably under Captain Schelle. There were no strange occurrences, and there was no evidence of a ghost. In fact, all went smoothly until May 1918, when the ghost returned, this time exhibiting a vindictive streak.

13   The first to feel its vengeance was Master Gunner Erich Eberhardt. A veteran of U-boats, not given to emotional outbursts of any kind, Gunner Eberhardt one day made a mad, panic-stricken dash into

A German U-boat is stranded on the coast of England after surrendering during World War I.

the control room. He was so wild that he had to be pinioned by the boat's guards. He kept babbling, "I've seen the ghost—an officer standing near the bow torpedo tubes. He brushed past me and disappeared!"

14 It took several crewmen to subdue the normally imperturbable gunner. Eberhardt was locked in the boat's tiny brig. When he was released hours later, having apparently recovered, he suddenly snatched a knife from a guard and killed himself on the spot.

15 Shortly after that incident, the U-65 surfaced to recharge its batteries. That was when Chief Petty Officer Richard Meyer, a close friend of the captain's, was swept over the side. His body was never recovered.

16 Officer Meyer's death spelled the end of the U-65's fighting efficiency. For the remainder of the patrol, the crew spent all its time trying to avoid, rather than engage, the enemy. Nevertheless, the boat was eventually hit by enemy shell fire and forced to limp back to Bruges for repairs.

17 As soon as the U-65 had tied up, an enraged Admiral Schroeder stormed on board. Wasting no time on explanations, he immediately relieved Captain Schelle of his command and had the entire crew transferred to other boats in the fleet. When the U-65 put out to sea again, in June 1918, it had a new captain and all new officers and crew.

18 The manner in which the U-65 met its end is quite as mystifying as the ghostly incidents that plagued it from the start. An American boat discovered the ill-starred U-boat lying on its side at sea on the morning of July 10, 1918. The American boat stood off for hours, its captain suspicious that the U-65 was a decoy, ready to explode should some unsuspecting enemy vessel close in to investigate. Finally, after hours of studying the U-boat that wallowed gently in the North Atlantic swells, the American captain gave his order: "Sink her. Ready all forward torpedo tubes!"

19 No sooner had he given that order than the U-65 was racked from within by a series of furious explosions. It broke into pieces and slipped to its watery grave. The American captain later reported that moments before the explosions he saw someone standing near the bow of the U-boat. It was, he said, the figure of a German naval officer dressed in a greatcoat, his arms folded across his chest.

20 "The War to End All Wars," as World War I was called, ended on November 11, 1918, with the Allies as victors. Since then a number of investigations, some formal, others informal, have been undertaken regarding the U-65. No satisfactory explanation for any of the strange events that took place on the boat has ever been uncovered.

If you have been timed while reading this article, enter your reading time below. Then turn to the Words-per-Minute Table on page 195 and look up your reading speed (words per minute). Enter your reading speed on the graph on page 196.

Reading Time: Lesson 17

_____ : _____
Minutes   Seconds

A | Finding the Main Idea

One statement below expresses the main idea of the article. One statement is too general, or too broad. The other statement explains only part of the article; it is too narrow. Label the statements using the following key:

M—Main Idea   **B—Too Broad**   **N—Too Narrow**

_____ 1. Several people reported seeing a ghost aboard the U-65, a German submarine used in World War I.

_____ 2. A great number of strange and tragic events took place aboard a German submarine.

_____ 3. Tragic events and reported sightings of ghosts plagued a German U-boat right up to its mysterious end.

_____ Score 15 points for a correct M answer.

_____ Score 5 points for each correct B or N answer.

_____ **Total Score:** Finding the Main Idea

B | Recalling Facts

How well do you remember the facts in the article? Put an X in the box next to the answer that correctly completes each statement about the article.

1. The German U-boats were built in
   - ☐ a. Belgium.
   - ☐ b. France.
   - ☐ c. Germany.

2. Problems started on the U-65
   - ☐ a. when it made its first dive.
   - ☐ b. while it was being built.
   - ☐ c. on launching day.

3. A ghost was first sighted on board the U-65 right after
   - ☐ a. a torpedo explosion.
   - ☐ b. it was launched.
   - ☐ c. its first war patrol.

4. The purpose of an exorcism is to
   - ☐ a. bless the ship before it goes to sea.
   - ☐ b. drive away evil spirits.
   - ☐ c. bring good luck.

5. The U-65 sank
   - ☐ a. when it was torpedoed by an American submarine.
   - ☐ b. as a result of unexplained explosions.
   - ☐ c. after the war ended.

Score 5 points for each correct answer.

_____ **Total Score:** Recalling Facts

C | Making Inferences

When you combine your own experience and information from a text to draw a conclusion that is not directly stated in that text, you are making an inference. Below are five statements that may or may not be inferences based on information in the article. Label the statements using the following key:

C—Correct Inference   **F—Faulty Inference**

_____ 1. In the first half of World War I, Germany was winning.

_____ 2. Admiral Schroeder finally agreed that the U-65 was haunted.

_____ 3. The U-65 was a total failure as a weapon.

_____ 4. A series of strange events aboard the U-65, particularly the death of Chief Petty Officer Meyer, affected Captain Schelle deeply.

_____ 5. Germany lost World War I largely because of the events that occurred on the U-65.

Score 5 points for each correct answer.

_____ **Total Score:** Making Inferences

D | Using Words Precisely

Each numbered sentence below contains an underlined word or phrase from the article. Following the sentence are three definitions. One definition is closest to the meaning of the underlined word. One definition is opposite or nearly opposite. Label those two definitions using the following key. Do not label the remaining definition.

C—Closest   O—Opposite or Nearly Opposite

1. Stories of that sort can quickly <u>demoralize</u> the crew of any warship.

_____ a. encourage

_____ b. weaken the spirit

_____ c. confuse

2. Then he <u>broached</u> the subject of the ghost.

_____ a. put aside

_____ b. wrote about

_____ c. brought up

3. After <u>denouncing</u> all talk of jinxed boats and ghosts as "superstitious nonsense," the admiral spent a night on board the U-65.

_____ a. condemning

_____ b. describing

_____ c. praising

4. It took several crewmen to subdue the normally <u>imperturbable</u> gunner.

_____ a. excitable

_____ b. cool-headed

_____ c. tardy

5. For the remainder of the patrol, the crew spent all its time trying to avoid, rather than <u>engage</u>, the enemy.

_____ a. talk to

_____ b. fight

_____ c. run away from

_____ Score 3 points for each correct C answer.

_____ Score 2 points for each correct O answer.

_____ **Total Score:** Using Words Precisely

Enter the four total scores in the spaces below, and add them together to find your Reading Comprehension Score. Then record your score on the graph on page 197.

Score	Question Type	Lesson 17
_____	Finding the Main Idea	
_____	Recalling Facts	
_____	Making Inferences	
_____	Using Words Precisely	
_____	**Reading Comprehension Score**	

Author's Approach

Put an X in the box next to the correct answer.

1. The author uses the first sentence of the article to
   - ☐ a. inform the reader about when the events took place.
   - ☐ b. inform the reader about the events in World War I.
   - ☐ c. compare the Germans to the Allies in World War I.

2. In this article, "the tide was beginning to turn against the Germans" means
   - ☐ a. the tide was causing German U-boats to become stuck underwater.
   - ☐ b. the Germans were beginning to lose the war.
   - ☐ c. German sailors on the U-boats were being swept overboard by rough seas.

3. What does the author imply by saying "When [Erich Eberhardt] was released hours later, having apparently recovered, he suddenly snatched a knife from a guard and killed himself on the spot"?
   - ☐ a. The ghost told Eberhardt to kill himself.
   - ☐ b. Eberhardt meant to kill the guard.
   - ☐ c. Eberhardt had not really recovered from the terror of seeing a ghost.

4. The author probably wrote this article in order to
   - ☐ a. describe the warships used during World War I.
   - ☐ b. tell the reader about a German U-boat that seemed jinxed.
   - ☐ c. explain how Germany lost World War I.

_____ Number of correct answers

Record your personal assessment of your work on the Critical Thinking Chart on page 198.

CRITICAL THINKING

Summarizing and Paraphrasing

Follow the directions provided for question 1. Put an X in the box next to the correct answer for question 2.

1. Look for the important ideas and events in paragraphs 10 and 11. Summarize those paragraphs in one or two sentences.

_____

_____

_____

2. Choose the sentence that correctly restates the following sentence from the article:

   "The American boat stood off for hours, its captain suspicious that the U-65 was a decoy, ready to explode should some unsuspecting enemy vessel close in to investigate."

   ☐ a. The captain of the American boat was afraid that the U-65 might explode if he went in to investigate it.

   ☐ b. The captain of the American boat wanted to wait until an enemy vessel torpedoed the U-65.

   ☐ c. The captain was afraid that an enemy vessel would investigate the U-65 and torpedo the American boat.

   _____ Number of correct answers

   Record your personal assessment of your work on the Critical Thinking Chart on page 198.

Critical Thinking

Put an X in the box next to the correct answer for questions 1, 2, and 5. Follow the directions provided for questions 3 and 4.

1. Which of the following statements from the article is an opinion rather than a fact?

   ☐ a. "The enormously successful U-boats were Germany's chief weapon in the war."

   ☐ b. "I'm sure it's just imagination."

   ☐ c. "Allied bombers struck Bruges in a lightning-fast raid, killing, among hundreds of others, the captain of the U-65."

2. From what Admiral Schroeder said and did, you can predict that he

   ☐ a. apologized to those who had survived the U-65 after he realized that the boat was jinxed.

   ☐ b. resigned his position after the U-65 met its mysterious end.

   ☐ c. never believed that the U-65 was haunted, even after its mysterious destruction.

3. Choose from the letters below to correctly complete the following statement. Write the letters on the lines.

   In the article, _____ and _____ are different.

   a. the manner in which the officer died on U-65's launching day

   b. the manner in which Erich Eberhardt died on the U-65

   c. the manner in which Richard Meyer died on the U-65

CRITICAL THINKING

4. Think about cause-effect relationships in the article. Fill in the blanks in the cause-effect chart, drawing from the letters below.

Cause	Effect
Sailors are superstitious.	_____
_____	Eberhardt had to be locked in the brig.
_____	U-65 went back to Bruges for repairs.

   a. He was panic-stricken after seeing what he thought was a ghost.

   b. It was hit by enemy shell fire while on patrol.

   c. The crew of the U-65 was terrified after the boat got stuck underwater on its first dive.

5. If you were an officer in the navy, how could you use the information in the article to convince your crew that a ship wasn't haunted?

   ☐ a. Spend a night on the ship to prove that there are no ghosts on board.

   ☐ b. Imprison anyone who claims to have seen a ghost.

   ☐ c. Warn the crew that anyone who even mentions ghosts will be dealt with severely.

_____ Number of correct answers

Record your personal assessment of your work on the Critical Thinking Chart on page 198.

Personal Response

What was most surprising or interesting to you about this article?

_____

_____

_____

_____

_____

Self-Assessment

The part I found most difficult about the article was

_____

_____

_____

I found this difficult because

_____

_____

_____

_____

CRITICAL THINKING

LADY IN BLACK

On a cold winter night in 1862, a Union soldier shivered in the frigid night air outside Fort Warren. He disliked night patrol at the fort, but he had no choice in the matter. Like all soldiers, he did what he was told. He gazed out at Boston Harbor and gave a melancholy sigh. He hoped that the war between the states would soon be over so that he could return to his family.

2   As the guard turned to make his return trip along the fort's stockade, he suddenly felt two hands around his neck. Struggling to free himself, he whirled around to confront his attacker and nearly fainted from shock. Facing him was a woman shrouded in black and surrounded by a shimmering halo of eerie light. Her face looked oddly familiar, but before he could remember where he had seen her before, she vanished.

3   "No one will believe this," the soldier muttered to himself, and he was right. At first his story met with jeers from his comrades. However, when the apparition returned night after night, startling one guard after another, the soldiers stopped laughing. It seemed that Fort Warren was haunted by a lady in black.

Fort Warren on Georges Island in Boston Harbor was used as a prison for Confederate soldiers during the Civil War.

4   Sarah Lanier tried unsuccessfully to hold back the tears as she waved good-bye to her husband. She and Andrew had grown up together in the little town of Crawfordville, Georgia, and had been childhood sweethearts. Now, only forty-eight hours after their wedding, Andrew was leaving to fight in the Civil War. Like thousands of other young southern men, Lieutenant Lanier had volunteered to fight in the Confederate Army.

5   Would Sarah ever see Andrew again? She tried not to think about it. Not the type to sit and brood over things beyond her control, she vowed to keep herself busy. She would do her part for the war effort by volunteering at the local hospital, and she would pray for her husband's safe return.

6   Andrew wrote often, which was some consolation to Sarah. But less than a month after his departure, she received a startling letter. Andrew wrote that he had been captured and was being held prisoner. He was imprisoned along with six hundred other Confederate soldiers, in the Corridor of Dungeons at Fort Warren, on Georges Island, off the coast of Boston, Massachusetts.

7   At least he's still alive, Sarah thought with relief, as she responded vaguely to the sympathy of her family and friends. Already a plan was forming in her mind. She would not sit idle while Andrew suffered in a northern jail. She would go to Boston and try to secure his release.

8   Horrified at Sarah's plan, her family and friends tried to discourage her. Young southern ladies simply did not travel without chaperones, even in the best of times. Now, with the country at war, she would be in grave danger. Besides, they counseled, her chances of succeeding in freeing her husband were nearly nonexistent.

9   Refusing to listen to advice, Sarah booked passage on a blockade runner that would take her to Hull, Massachusetts, a seacoast town just a few miles south of Boston. There she would stay with friends who would help her carry out her plans.

10   Sarah reached her destination two and a half months later. Overlooking Boston Harbor, Hull was the perfect location from which to study Fort Warren, which lay about seven miles off the mainland in Boston Harbor. Using a telescope, Sarah was able to identify the Corridor of Dungeons, where her husband was imprisoned. She studied the height of the prison walls and their distance from the shore, and noted where the guards were stationed and when they patrolled.

11   On a bitter January night, with sleet falling relentlessly, Sarah put her plan into action. Her hair cut short, and wearing a man's dark suit, she climbed into a small boat and was rowed by her friends across Hingham Bay into Boston Harbor. After she had been dropped off at Georges Island, Sarah crouched in the surf, waiting for the guards to pass by. She timed their patrol a second time for good measure; there was no room for mistakes now. Sarah calculated that she had a minute and a half to scramble the two or three hundred feet across the beach and into the bushes at the base of the stockade.

After the guards passed again, she would have another ninety seconds to clamber over the stockade and drop into the courtyard of the fort.

12   Thankful for the sleet that helped to camouflage her, Sarah made it across the wet sand to the bushes. Her heart thudded as she waited for the guards to pass. Then she scaled the stockade and landed with a thump on the other side. She was inside the fort, with her husband only yards away in the Corridor of Dungeons.

13   After checking to be certain there were no sentries within earshot, Sarah began to whistle a tune she was sure her husband

The Guard House at Fort Warren

would recognize—the melody of an old folk song they had sung together since childhood. Failing to get an answer, Sarah whistled the tune again, but still she heard no answer.

14　For the first time since she resolved to rescue her husband, Sarah began to have doubts about her scheme. While she was traveling north, there had been no way she could have gotten word from Andrew. He might be sick, or perhaps he had even been transferred to another prison. In a last desperate attempt, Sarah whistled a third time. She waited what seemed like an eternity. Then she heard faintly, mingled with the patter of falling sleet, the softly whistled notes of the old folk tune. Andrew was there!

15　Sarah watched as a crude ladder made from blankets tied together came hurtling over the wall. Grasping hold, she was hoisted over the wall and into her husband's waiting arms. The other prisoners listened with amazement as Sarah related her incredible story. Then from under her clothing she pulled a bundle containing a pick, a shovel, a pistol, and a box of ammunition. With the tools they could tunnel under the walls of the fort to freedom.

16　But the prisoners suggested another course of action: instead of escaping, they wanted to tunnel into the courtyard near the guard post, surprise the guard, and seize the fort. From there, they might even occupy the city of Boston! They went ahead with that plan.

17　Days and then weeks passed, and little by little the tunnel grew. Sarah and the men scattered some of the excavated dirt outside the fortress walls; the rest they hid in their blankets and clothing. Finally they reached a point that they determined was in the center of the courtyard. But when they swung the pick to break through to the surface, the metal clanged against stone wall; they had miscalculated. Alerted by the sound, a sentry called out the garrison, and the guards soon discovered the tunnel and the prisoners' plan.

18　But the Union soldiers knew nothing about Sarah Lanier, who remained hidden in the tunnel as the Confederate prisoners were rounded up and counted. At the proper moment, she intended to sneak up behind the colonel and catch him unaware, giving the prisoners the chance to turn on the guards and take the fort. Unfortunately for Sarah and the Confederate soldiers, the daring plan backfired. When Sarah held a pistol to the colonel's back, he calmly ordered his troops to surround her. Confused and hesitant, Sarah allowed the colonel to snatch her pistol, causing it to go off. She watched in horror as Andrew crumpled to the ground, killed instantly by the stray bullet.

19　Sobbing, Sarah ran to her husband. The Union soldiers were astonished to discover that she was a woman. Nevertheless, she was a spy and must receive the established punishment for spying: death by hanging.

20　The colonel must have felt some pity for the courageous woman, for he granted Sarah's last request. She expressed a wish to be hanged in clothes befitting a southern lady, so the colonel provided a long black robe that he found in the fort.

21　Wearing the black robe, and managing a brave smile, Sarah walked to the gallows on the morning of February 2, 1862. Several hours later, her body was cut down and buried next to that of her husband.

22　Sarah's body may have been put to rest, but it seems that her spirit was not. Since her first appearance to sentries patrolling the stockade at Fort Warren seven weeks after her hanging, the Lady in Black has appeared many times. One sentry who patrolled the fort during World War II was literally frightened out of his wits by the apparition; to this day he remains in a mental hospital.

23　Today Fort Warren is no longer used as a prison. It is a historic site and a popular tourist attraction. The bodies of Sarah and Andrew Lanier have long since been removed to Georgia, yet, they say that late at night the ghost of the Lady in Black continues to haunt the old fort that sits in Boston Harbor.

If you have been timed while reading this article, enter your reading time below. Then turn to the Words-per-Minute Table on page 195 and look up your reading speed (words per minute). Enter your reading speed on the graph on page 196.

Reading Time: Lesson 18

_____ : _____
Minutes   Seconds

A Finding the Main Idea

One statement below expresses the main idea of the article. One statement is too general, or too broad. The other statement explains only part of the article; it is too narrow. Label the statements using the following key:

M—Main Idea   B—Too Broad   N—Too Narrow

_____ 1. Sarah Lanier was hanged when she was found to be a spy.

_____ 2. A ghost shrouded in black supposedly haunts a fort that sits on an island in Boston Harbor.

_____ 3. It is said that the ghost of a southern woman who was hanged as a spy during the Civil War still haunts the prison where she was killed.

_____ Score 15 points for a correct M answer.

_____ Score 5 points for each correct B or N answer.

_____ **Total Score:** Finding the Main Idea

B Recalling Facts

How well do you remember the facts in the article? Put an X in the box next to the answer that correctly completes each statement about the article.

1. Fort Warren is situated
   ☐ a. in the Corridor of Dungeons.
   ☐ b. on Georges Island.
   ☐ c. in Boston, Massachusetts.

2. To let Andrew know she was outside the prison walls, Sarah
   ☐ a. sang a childhood song.
   ☐ b. whistled an old folk tune.
   ☐ c. threw a rock over the wall.

3. The Confederate prisoners decided to
   ☐ a. dig a tunnel under the wall of the fort to the outside.
   ☐ b. try to seize the fort.
   ☐ c. dig a tunnel to Boston.

4. Sarah's last request was to be
   ☐ a. hanged in clothes fit for a lady.
   ☐ b. buried next to her husband.
   ☐ c. hanged rather than shot.

5. Sarah and Andrew are now buried
   ☐ a. at Fort Warren.
   ☐ b. in Georgia.
   ☐ c. in Boston.

Score 5 points for each correct answer.

_____ **Total Score:** Recalling Facts

C Making Inferences

When you combine your own experience and information from a text to draw a conclusion that is not directly stated in that text, you are making an inference. Below are five statements that may or may not be inferences based on information in the article. Label the statements using the following key:

C—Correct Inference   F—Faulty Inference

_____ 1. Spies today are still usually punished by hanging.

_____ 2. Fort Warren is no longer used as a prison because too many guards were badly frightened by the ghost of the Lady in Black.

_____ 3. Had they followed Sarah's plan, the Confederate prisoners would have had a good chance of escaping.

_____ 4. The Confederate prisoners cared more about their duty as soldiers than about their personal safety.

_____ 5. Andrew was prepared for Sarah's arrival at the prison.

Score 5 points for each correct answer.

_____ **Total Score:** Making Inferences

D Using Words Precisely

Each numbered sentence below contains an underlined word or phrase from the article. Following the sentence are three definitions. One definition is closest to the meaning of the underlined word. One definition is opposite or nearly opposite. Label those two definitions using the following key. Do not label the remaining definition.

C—Closest   O—Opposite or Nearly Opposite

1. He gazed out at Boston Harbor and gave a <u>melancholy</u> sigh.

_____ a. gloomy

_____ b. lighthearted

_____ c. loud

2. Struggling to free himself, he whirled around to <u>confront</u> his attacker and nearly fainted from shock.

_____ a. scare

_____ b. face

_____ c. avoid

3. At first his story met with <u>jeers</u> from his comrades.

_____ a. wonder

_____ b. mockery

_____ c. cheers

4. Not the type to sit and <u>brood</u> over things beyond her control, she vowed to keep herself busy.

_____ a. discuss

_____ b. rejoice

_____ c. worry

5. For the first time since she <u>resolved</u> to rescue her husband, Sarah began to have doubts about her scheme.

_____ a. decided

_____ b. asked others

_____ c. hesitated

_____ Score 3 points for each correct C answer.

_____ Score 2 points for each correct O answer.

_____ **Total Score:** Using Words Precisely

Enter the four total scores in the spaces below, and add them together to find your Reading Comprehension Score. Then record your score on the graph on page 197.

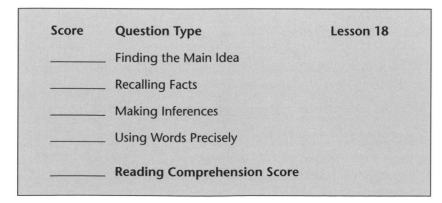

Score	Question Type	Lesson 18
_____	Finding the Main Idea	
_____	Recalling Facts	
_____	Making Inferences	
_____	Using Words Precisely	
_____	**Reading Comprehension Score**	

Author's Approach

Put an X in the box next to the correct answer.

1. What does the author mean by the statement "Her heart thudded as she waited for the guards to pass"?

☐ a. Sarah was tired from running.

☐ b. Sarah had heart trouble.

☐ c. Sarah was afraid of being seen and captured.

2. What is the author's purpose in writing "Lady in Black"?

☐ a. To persuade the reader that Sarah Lanier was treated unfairly

☐ b. To tell the reader about Sarah Lanier and her attempt to rescue her husband

☐ c. To emphasize the similarities between Union soldiers and Confederate soldiers

3. Which of the following statements from the article best describes Sarah Lanier's attitude toward life?

☐ a. "For the first time since she resolved to rescue her husband, Sarah began to have doubts about her scheme."

☐ b. "Sobbing, Sarah ran to her husband."

☐ c. "She would not sit idle while Andrew suffered in a northern jail."

4. From the statements below, choose those that you believe the author would agree with.

☐ a. The Union colonel admired and pitied Sarah.

☐ b. The Confederate prisoners would have escaped if Sarah had shot the colonel.

☐ c. Sarah was prepared to do anything to rescue her husband.

_____ Number of correct answers

Record your personal assessment of your work on the Critical Thinking Chart on page 198.

CRITICAL THINKING

Summarizing and Paraphrasing

Put an X in the box next to the correct answer.

_____ Number of correct answers

Record your personal assessment of your work on the Critical Thinking Chart on page 198.

1. Below are summaries of the article. Choose the summary that says all the most important things about the article but in the fewest words.

☐ a. Before Sarah Lanier was executed for trying to free her husband, she asked to be allowed to wear a black dress. Since her death, an apparition dressed in black has been seen at Fort Warren from time to time.

☐ b. Sarah Lanier tried to rescue her husband, a Confederate soldier, who was being held in a Union prison. Andrew died during the escape attempt, and Sarah was later executed. Since then, Sarah's ghost is said to haunt the prison.

☐ c. Soon after Andrew Lanier, a Confederate soldier, went off to fight during the Civil War, he was captured and locked up in a Union prison near Boston. His wife, Sarah, snuck into the prison to try to help him escape. After their plan was discovered, Andrew was accidentally shot and Sarah was later executed. Ever since then, her ghost has haunted the prison.

2. Read the statement about the article below. Then read the paraphrase of that statement. Choose the reason that best tells why the paraphrase does not say the same thing as the statement.

Statement: Even though the bodies of Sarah and Andrew Lanier have been removed, some people say that Sarah's ghost, dressed in black, still haunts the old fort in Boston Harbor.

Paraphrase: The bodies of Sarah and Andrew Lanier were transferred to Georgia years ago, but some people visiting the popular tourist site in Boston Harbor claim that they have seen the Lady in Black walking around the historic old fort.

☐ a. Paraphrase says too much.

☐ b. Paraphrase doesn't say enough.

☐ c. Paraphrase doesn't agree with the statement about the article.

Critical Thinking

Follow the directions provided for questions 1, 3, and 4. Put an X in the box next to the correct answer for questions 2 and 5.

1. For each statement below, write O if it expresses an opinion and write F if it expresses a fact.

_____ a. A bullet from Sarah's gun killed her husband.

_____ b. Sarah brought tools and ammunition to the prison.

_____ c. Sarah was the bravest woman in the Confederacy.

2. Judging by the events in the article, you can predict that the following will happen next:

☐ a. from time to time, people will continue to spot Sarah's ghost in the fort.

☐ b. southern sympathizers will try to capture the fort to set Sarah's ghost free.

☐ c. tourists will stop visiting the fort because they are too afraid they might meet Sarah's ghost.

3. Choose from the letters below to correctly complete the following statement. Write the letters on the lines.

On the positive side, _____, but on the negative side _____.

a. they both died at the prison

b. Sarah and Andrew were reunited

c. Sarah's ghost still haunts the old prison

4. Read paragraph 22. Then choose from the letters below to correctly complete the following statement. Write the letters on the lines.

According to paragraph 22, _____ because _____.

a. a sentry at the fort is in a mental hospital

b. he patrolled during World War II

c. he saw the Lady in Black

5. What did you have to do to answer question 1?

☐ a. find a summary (synthesized information)

☐ b. find a cause (why something happened)

☐ c. find a fact (something that you can prove is true)

_____ Number of correct answers

Record your personal assessment of your work on the Critical Thinking Chart on page 198.

Personal Response

I know how Sarah Lanier feels because

_____

_____

_____

Self-Assessment

When reading the article, I was having trouble with

_____

_____

_____

_____

CRITICAL THINKING

GHOSTS IN THE CAPITAL

It is easy to see why Washington, D.C., is considered one supernatural city. Ghosts are said to inhabit many of the buildings there. According to a popular legend, a ghost resides in the White House itself. Abraham Lincoln's wife Mary swore she often heard the ghost of Thomas Jefferson playing the violin. The Capitol Building, too, has its ghosts. America's sixth president, John Quincy Adams, suffered a fatal heart attack in this building. He is said to return from time to time to speak to members of Congress.

2   Perhaps the most haunted house in the city is the Octagon House. This big old mansion was built in 1800 by Colonel John Tayloe. Tayloe was a Virginian who had been one of the heroes of the American Revolution. As the new nation grew, he decided he wanted a home in Washington, D.C. He chose as his architect Dr. William Thornton, the man who had designed the Capitol. The result of Thornton's work is a six-sided house that for some reason came to be called the Octagon House.

The Octagon House in Washington, D. C., is often referred to as the second White House because President James Madison lived there during the War of 1812. The ghost of his wife, Dolley, is said to haunt the house.

3   Tayloe moved into the Octagon House with his wife and two daughters. For a time they lived happily. They held grand parties, entertaining all the important people of the day. But as Colonel Tayloe's daughters grew older, tension developed in the family. The older daughter fell in love with an Englishman, a man Colonel Tayloe did not like. After a heated argument with her father, the girl ran up the central stairway toward the top of the house. As she reached the second landing, something happened. No one knows whether she slipped or deliberately threw herself over the banister, but she fell two stories to her death, landing in a heap at the bottom of the stairs.

4   The Tayloes' troubles didn't end there. Some time later, their second daughter also picked a man Colonel Tayloe felt was unsuitable. Despite her father's objections, this younger daughter went ahead with her marriage plans. Soon after the wedding, she returned to her parents' house to see if she could persuade the colonel to accept her new husband. He refused. Again there is confusion surrounding the exact events. Somehow, though, the girl met her father on the stairs soon after arguing about her new husband. Perhaps she stepped backward to avoid her father; perhaps he, in his anger, gave her a small push. In any case,

the girl, like her older sister, tumbled over the banister to her death.

5   Colonel Tayloe was devastated. Both his beautiful daughters were gone. Still, the Tayloes kept their grief private and continued to host lavish parties in their house. When the British set fire to the White House during the War of 1812, the Tayloes graciously invited President James Madison and his wife, Dolley, to stay in the Octagon House.

6   Music, dancing, and feasts did little to comfort Colonel Tayloe, however, and a few years after his daughters' deaths, he too passed away. From then on, the house seemed to attract tragedy. Stories circulated about a young servant who had supposedly been killed by her lover and hidden between the walls of the house. Another servant, who rejected the advances of a British naval officer, was rumored to have jumped to her death from the same stairway that the Tayloe girls fell from.

7   During the Civil War, the Octagon House was used as a makeshift hospital for wounded soldiers. Before the war ended, many young men drew their last breaths in the house. At one point, a gambler owned the Octagon House. One night he heard an intruder entering his room and, recognizing a man he had cheated out of money, reached for his gun. But the

gambler was too late. He was shot to death before he could raise his pistol.

8   As each death occurred, the Octagon House seemed to get more and more gloomy. People who went there began to tell tales of strange occurrences in the

The staircase of the Octagon House has been the scene of three tragic deaths. The ghosts of the Tayloe girls are said to hover near these stairs.

building. Some swore they saw the ghost of a short woman wearing a feathered turban. That description fits Dolley Madison, who always wore a distinctive feathered turban when she entertained. Other visitors have seen or heard different ghosts. Some have seen the gambler reaching for his gun; others have heard the sobs of dying Civil War soldiers.

9   The primary ghosts of the Octagon House, however, appear to be the three unhappy members of the Tayloe family. Again and again, the footsteps of Colonel Tayloe have been heard as he walks disconsolately through the halls, sometimes rattling his sword in despair. The girls, meanwhile, hover near the stairs, creating a cold draft and sometimes screaming in pain.

10   By the 1960s, the Octagon House had been taken over by the American Institute of Architects. The staffers who worked there were not the sort to believe in ghosts, yet many of them admitted to witnessing odd events during their time in the building. One of these people was Mrs. Belma May, the office supervisor. Sometimes when she was alone in the building with the windows closed, she saw the chandelier start to swing. She also found footprints in the dust on the landing at the top of the stairs. The footprints looked to her as though someone had tiptoed to the edge of the banister and jumped off.

11   Mrs. May often felt a chill when she neared the spot at the bottom of the stairs where the Tayloe girls had died. Others felt similar blasts of cold air around that spot. When walking up the stairs, porters and caretakers reported feeling as if someone were following them. Whenever they looked around, however, no one was there.

12   Later, Alric H. Clay was put in charge of the building. Once, in the middle of the night, he received a call from the police alerting him that all the lights in the Octagon House were on. Clay knew he had been the last one to leave the building that night, and he was sure he had turned out the lights before leaving. Since he was the only one with a key, he worried that burglars might have broken in. To his relief, the police checked the building thoroughly and found nothing out of place. They turned off all the lights and made sure the doors were locked when they left. At 7:00 A.M., police officers swung by the Octagon House again. Once again, all the lights in the building were on.

13   In 1962, *Life* magazine published an article on the Octagon House. The article reported that visitors often saw a shadow at the foot of the deadly staircase. Seven years later, author Hans Holzer decided to check out the house for himself. Holzer was a well-known author who had written more than 30 books on psychic phenomena. When he went to the Octagon House, he took with him Ethel Johnson Meyers, a psychic who knew nothing of the building's history. As Holzer watched, Meyers moved to the stairway and announced that for some reason the stairs frightened her. Nonetheless, she began to climb them. As she did so, she described a sudden and intense pain in her head. "I'm holding onto my head," she said, adding that it "hurts, very badly." A bit later she cried out, "I've got to put my hand up, always to my head, *it hurts so.*"

14   As Meyers climbed higher up the stairs, she suddenly turned around. "Don't push me!" she cried out.

15   Later, Meyers gave Holzer her assessment of the Octagon House, which he included in his book titled *The Ghosts That Walk in Washington*. She said that she sensed several "layers" of psychic energy in the house. "This house is terribly psychic, as it were," she said. "It is as if I have been able to find the easiest possible connections with a lot of people through what has been done here, psychically. There's a psychic circle around this place. From the past."

If you have been timed while reading this article, enter your reading time below. Then turn to the Words-per-Minute Table on page 195 and look up your reading speed (words per minute). Enter your reading speed on the graph on page 196.

Reading Time: **Lesson 19**

_____ : _____
Minutes   Seconds

Finding the Main Idea

One statement below expresses the main idea of the article. One statement is too general, or too broad. The other statement explains only part of the article; it is too narrow. Label the statements using the following key:

M—Main Idea   B—Too Broad   N—Too Narrow

_____ 1. People believe that ghosts inhabit many of the buildings in Washington, D.C.

_____ 2. The Tayloe girls fell to their death from the central staircase in the Octagon House.

_____ 3. The ghosts of the Tayloes and others who died in the Octagon House make that building one of the most haunted in Washington, D.C.

_____ Score 15 points for a correct M answer.

_____ Score 5 points for each correct B or N answer.

_____ **Total Score:** Finding the Main Idea

 Recalling Facts

How well do you remember the facts in the article? Put an X in the box next to the answer that correctly completes each statement about the article.

1. Colonel John Tayloe was
  □ a. a hero of the Civil War.
  □ b. a hero of the American Revolution.
  □ c. the man who had designed the Capitol.

2. Both of the Tayloe daughters died when they
  □ a. were killed by their lovers.
  □ b. were shot by an intruder.
  □ c. fell from the staircase in their home.

3. During the Civil War, the Octagon House
  □ a. housed President James Madison and his wife Dolley.
  □ b. was home to a gambler.
  □ c. was used as a hospital for wounded soldiers.

4. At the bottom of the stairs in the Octagon House, some people have
  □ a. felt a cold draft.
  □ b. seen the gambler reaching for his gun.
  □ c. heard the sobs of dying Civil War soldiers.

5. When Hans Holzer went to the Octagon House, he
  □ a. turned off the lights.
  □ b. studied the building for a report that would appear in Life magazine.
  □ c. took a psychic with him.

Score 5 points for each correct answer.

_____ **Total Score:** Recalling Facts

C Making Inferences

When you combine your own experience and information from a text to draw a conclusion that is not directly stated in that text, you are making an inference. Below are five statements that may or may not be inferences based on information in the article. Label the statements using the following key:

C—Correct Inference   F—Faulty Inference

_____ 1. John Tayloe was a permissive, kind-hearted father.

_____ 2. Tayloe killed his daughters on purpose.

_____ 3. Whoever named the Octagon House did not know the meaning of the word *octagon*.

_____ 4. Everyone who visits Washington, D.C., sees a ghost in one of the city's buildings.

_____ 5. After the police turned off the lights in the Octagon House, Alric Clay went to the building and turned them back on.

Score 5 points for each correct answer.

_____ **Total Score:** Making Inferences

D Using Words Precisely

Each numbered sentence below contains an underlined word or phrase from the article. Following the sentence are three definitions. One definition is closest to the meaning of the underlined word. One definition is opposite or nearly opposite. Label those two definitions using the following key. Do not label the remaining definition.

C—Closest   O—Opposite or Nearly Opposite

1. No one knows whether she slipped or <u>deliberately</u> threw herself over the banister, but she fell two stories to her death, landing in a heap at the bottom of the stairs.

_____ a. impossibly

_____ b. involuntarily

_____ c. intentionally

2. Colonel Tayloe was <u>devastated</u>.

_____ a. brokenhearted

_____ b. very happy

_____ c. very ill

3. During the Civil War, the Octagon House was used as a <u>makeshift</u> hospital for wounded soldiers.

_____ a. excellent

_____ b. permanent

_____ c. temporary

4. That description fits Dolley Madison, who always wore a <u>distinctive</u> feathered turban when she entertained.

_____ a. common

_____ b. ugly

_____ c. unique

5. Again and again, the footsteps of Colonel Tayloe have been heard as he walks <u>disconsolately</u> through the halls, sometimes rattling his sword in despair.

_____ a. quietly

_____ b. hopelessly

_____ c. joyfully

_____

_____ Score 3 points for each correct C answer.

_____ Score 2 points for each correct O answer.

_____ **Total Score:** Using Words Precisely

Enter the four total scores in the spaces below, and add them together to find your Reading Comprehension Score. Then record your score on the graph on page 197.

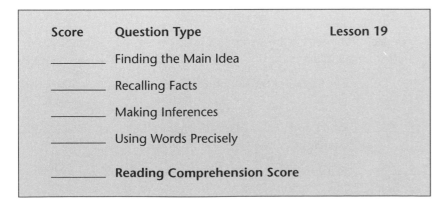

Score	Question Type	Lesson 19
_____	Finding the Main Idea	
_____	Recalling Facts	
_____	Making Inferences	
_____	Using Words Precisely	
_____	**Reading Comprehension Score**	

Author's Approach

Put an X in the box next to the correct answer.

1. The main purpose of the first paragraph is to

   ☐ a. convince the reader to visit Washington, D.C.

   ☐ b. tell the reader about some of the haunted buildings in Washington, D.C.

   ☐ c. compare Abraham Lincoln with Thomas Jefferson.

2. Which of the following statements from the article best describes Colonel John Tayloe's state of mind late in life?

   ☐ a. "Tayloe moved into the Octagon House with his wife and two daughters."

   ☐ b. "As the new nation grew, he decided he wanted a home in Washington, D.C."

   ☐ c. "Music, dancing, and feasts did little to comfort Colonel Tayloe, however, and a few years after his daughters' deaths, he too passed away."

3. From the statements below, choose those that you believe the author would agree with.

   ☐ a. Ethel Meyers had read about the hauntings at the Octagon House before she visited it.

   ☐ b. Colonel Tayloe greatly missed his daughters after they died.

   ☐ c. Many people who visit the Octagon House feel a supernatural presence in the building.

4. From the statement "Sometimes when she [Belva May] was alone in the building with the windows closed, she saw the chandelier start to swing," you can conclude that the author wants the reader to think that

☐ a.   unknown forces caused the chandelier to move.

☐ b.   strong winds caused the chandelier to move.

☐ c.   Mrs. May caused the chandelier to move.

_____ Number of correct answers

Record your personal assessment of your work on the Critical Thinking Chart on page 198.

Summarizing and Paraphrasing

Follow the directions provided for question 1. Put an X in the box next to the correct answer for question 2.

1. Look for the important ideas and events in paragraphs 3 and 4. Summarize those paragraphs in one or two sentences.

_____

_____

_____

2. Read the statement about the article below. Then read the paraphrase of that statement. Choose the reason that best tells why the paraphrase does not say the same thing as the statement.

Statement: Ethel Johnson Meyers, a psychic who knew nothing about the Octagon House's haunted history, climbed the stairs in the building, even though she claimed that something about them frightened her.

Paraphrase: Even though Meyers knew that something frightening had happened on the stairs in the Octagon House, she began climbing them.

☐ a.   Paraphrase says too much.

☐ b.   Paraphrase doesn't say enough.

☐ c.   Paraphrase doesn't agree with the statement about the article.

_____ Number of correct answers

Record your personal assessment of your work on the Critical Thinking Chart on page 198.

Critical Thinking

Follow the directions provided for questions 1, 3, and 4. Put an X in the box next to the correct answer for questions 2 and 5.

1. For each statement below, write O if it expresses an opinion or write F if it expresses a fact.

_____ a.   The Octagon House is the scariest building in Washington, D.C.

_____ b.   James and Dolley Madison lived in the Octagon House for a while after the White House was damaged by fire.

_____ c.   In 1962, Life magazine published an article that featured the Octagon House.

2. From what the article told about Colonel John Tayloe, you can predict that he would

  ☐ a. never have accepted his younger daughter's husband.

  ☐ b. have murdered his younger daughter's husband if he'd had the chance.

  ☐ c. have eventually persuaded his daughter to leave her husband and come back home.

3. Choose from the letters below to correctly complete the following statement. Write the letters on the lines.

In the article, _____ and _____ are alike.

  a. the circumstances of John Tayloe's death

  b. the circumstances of the younger Tayloe girl's death

  c. the circumstances of the older Tayloe girl's death

4. Read paragraph 5. Then choose from the letters below to correctly complete the following statement. Write the letters on the lines.

According to paragraph 5, _____ because _____.

  a. the White House had been damaged by fire

  b. the Tayloes gave lavish parties in their home

  c. the Tayloes invited President Madison and his wife to stay with them

5. What did you have to do to answer question 1?

  ☐ a. find a reason (why something is the way it is)

  ☐ b. find an opinion (what someone thinks about something)

  ☐ c. find a comparison (how things are the same)

> _____ Number of correct answers
>
> Record your personal assessment of your work on the Critical Thinking Chart on page 198.

Personal Response

I know how the Tayloe girls felt because

_____

_____

_____

_____

Self-Assessment

When reading the article, I was having trouble with

_____

_____

_____

_____

CRITICAL THINKING

THE SMURL HAUNTING

Jack and Janet Smurl stand in front of their haunted house in West Pittston, Pennsylvania.

Jack and Janet Smurl loved their new home. They knew the duplex at 328 Chase Street in West Pittston, Pennsylvania, needed some work, but they were handy at remodeling and looked forward to making improvements in the place. And with Jack's parents living in the other half of the house, the Smurls would have willing babysitters for their two young daughters. All in all, the family was happy and excited when they moved into the 75-year-old house on October 1, 1973.

2   For a while, life went smoothly, but after about 18 months, everything changed. Odd things began to happen. A stain suddenly appeared on their new carpeting, all the pipes in the house began to leak, and the TV burst into flames. One day Jack installed a brand new porcelain sink and bathtub in their bathroom. The next morning, he was shocked to see that both new fixtures had been badly scratched and clawed, as though some wild animal had been digging at them.

3   From then on, there was no end to the strange occurrences at 328 Chase Street. Claw marks appeared on freshly painted

surfaces around the house. Unplugged radios blared loud music. And the Smurls often heard drawers opening, toilets flushing, and empty rocking chairs rocking.

4   Jack and Janet realized that some kind of ghost was loose in their house, but they refused to be intimidated. They were a strong, religious family and were not about to be driven out of their beloved home. For a while, that brave attitude served them well. They managed to ignore many of the bizarre incidents that plagued them. They continued making improvements in the house. And in 1978, they added twin girls to their family.

5   By 1983, however, the Smurls were becoming scared and frustrated. Whatever presence was haunting them seemed to be getting more powerful. A nasty odor often permeated their home. And one day, when Janet was alone in the basement doing laundry, she heard her name being called over and over again.

6   Finally, violence erupted in the Smurls' house. A heavy kitchen light fixture fell from the ceiling, injuring their 14-year-old daughter. The family dog was lifted from the floor and flung against the wall. Janet was pulled from her bed one night and dragged across the floor. At this point, the Smurls sought help. Janet contacted

colleges around the country to see if any of them could help explain the phenomena. But no professor wanted any part of the Smurls and their strange tales. One even brushed Janet off by suggesting she had been watching too many horror movies.

7   At last, in January 1986, the Smurls heard about Ed and Lorraine Warren. The Warrens ran the New England Society for Psychic Research. They had investigated over 3,000 hauntings. In despair, the Smurls contacted them and asked for help.

8   For the next several months, the Warrens worked with the Smurls. The Warrens said they detected the presence of four spirits in the house. One was a harmless old woman, while another was a younger woman who was insane and often violent. A third was a man who possessed a great capacity for violence. And the fourth was a true demon, bent on destroying the family.

9   The Warrens weren't surprised that these four spirits had attached themselves to the Smurl family. Ed Warren explained that spirits often emerge in families with teenage children. "That's the classic pattern," he told Jack and Janet. "Puberty often brings on infestations. The demon is drawing on your daughters' emotional

turbulence, and now it's tapping into yours."

10   The Warrens tried to dispel the spirits using the power of religion. They recited prayers and played recordings of hymns

Ed and Lorraine Warren, of the New England Society for Psychic Research, tried to help the Smurls rid their house of ghosts.

throughout the house. Those tactics only seemed to anger the spirits, for the violence soon escalated. The Smurls asked church officials to help, but the officials declined. Like the college professors, most church leaders thought the Smurls were making everything up.

11   The Warrens eventually found a priest who was willing to help them. His name was Father Robert McKenna. He came into the home and offered blessings, recited prayers, and sprinkled each room with holy water. When those efforts failed to make any difference, the Smurls considered moving out of the house they loved so much. But the Warrens informed them that, in all likelihood, a move would do no good; the spirits would probably follow them wherever they went. To test that theory, Jack and Janet took their daughters on a camping trip. Sure enough, Jack's bed was ripped from the camper floor as he tried to sleep. The Smurls began to feel that there was no escape.

12   Desperate, they decided to go public with their story. They hoped the media attention might attract someone who could help them. And so, on August 17, 1986, the *Wilkes-Barre Sunday Independent* published an account of their ordeal. The Smurls soon found, however, that publicity made their lives more difficult. They were bombarded with phone calls from tabloid journalists. Their street became

crowded with curious spectators. The Catholic Church sent a priest to check out their house, but the spirits did not reveal themselves while the priest was present. So the Smurls found themselves no better off than they were before the newspaper story ran.

13   By 1988, the Smurls had written a book based on their experiences called *The Haunted*. In 1991, a movie version of the book was also made. By then, the home situation seemed a little better for Jack and Janet Smurl. The supernatural forces that had terrified them for years had finally faded away. Even so, the Smurls saw their case as a warning to all families. If spirits could attack their happy home, they reasoned, then perhaps no one was safe from the eerie forces of the dead. 🍃

If you have been timed while reading this article, enter your reading time below. Then turn to the Words-per-Minute Table on page 195 and look up your reading speed (words per minute). Enter your reading speed on the graph on page 196.

Reading Time: Lesson 20

_____ : _____
Minutes   Seconds

A | Finding the Main Idea

One statement below expresses the main idea of the article. One statement is too general, or too broad. The other statement explains only part of the article; it is too narrow. Label the statements using the following key:

M—Main Idea   **B—Too Broad**   **N—Too Narrow**

_____ 1. For years, the Smurl family was tormented by destructive, violent spirits.

_____ 2. Spirits often attach themselves to families with teenage children.

_____ 3. The Smurls' teenage daughter was injured when a heavy kitchen light fixture fell from the ceiling.

_____ Score 15 points for a correct M answer.

_____ Score 5 points for each correct B or N answer.

_____ **Total Score:** Finding the Main Idea

B | Recalling Facts

How well do you remember the facts in the article? Put an X in the box next to the answer that correctly completes each statement about the article.

1. The day after Jack Smurl installed a brand new porcelain sink and bathtub, both new fixtures
   - ☐ a. burst into flame.
   - ☐ b. began to leak.
   - ☐ c. looked as if they had been clawed.

2. When Janet was alone in the basement doing laundry,
   - ☐ a. she was dragged across the floor.
   - ☐ b. she heard her name being called over and over.
   - ☐ c. the family dog was flung against the wall.

3. The college professors Janet contacted for help
   - ☐ a. sprinkled each room of the house with holy water.
   - ☐ b. refused to help.
   - ☐ c. wrote a book about the Smurls' experiences.

4. Ed and Lorraine Warren detected the presence of
   - ☐ a. four spirits in the house.
   - ☐ b. 3,000 spirits in the house.
   - ☐ c. three spirits in the house.

5. In an effort to get away from the spirits, the Smurls
   - ☐ a. went on a camping trip.
   - ☐ b. published an account of their ordeal in the local newspaper.
   - ☐ c. made a movie based on their experiences.

Score 5 points for each correct answer.

_____ **Total Score:** Recalling Facts

C Making Inferences

When you combine your own experience and information from a text to draw a conclusion that is not directly stated in that text, you are making an inference. Below are five statements that may or may not be inferences based on information in the article. Label the statements using the following key:

C—Correct Inference   **F—Faulty Inference**

_____ 1. The book the Smurls wrote about their strange ordeal became a bestseller.

_____ 2. The Smurls' teenage daughters invited the spirits into their home.

_____ 3. The Smurls trusted the Warrens to tell them the truth.

_____ 4. The movie about the Smurls' experiences could be classified as a horror film.

_____ 5. The spirits haunting the Smurls' home were frightened by religious ceremonies.

Score 5 points for each correct answer.

_____ **Total Score:** Making Inferences

D Using Words Precisely

Each numbered sentence below contains an underlined word or phrase from the article. Following the sentence are three definitions. One definition is closest to the meaning of the underlined word. One definition is opposite or nearly opposite. Label those two definitions using the following key. Do not label the remaining definition.

C—Closest   **O—Opposite or Nearly Opposite**

1. Jack and Janet realized that some kind of ghost was loose in their house, but they refused to be intimidated.

_____ a. made bold

_____ b. frightened

_____ c. moved

2. Finally, violence erupted in the Smurls' home.

_____ a. believed

_____ b. died out

_____ c. broke out

3. "The demon is drawing on your daughters' emotional turbulence, and now it's tapping into yours."

_____ a. calm

_____ b. scars

_____ c. agitation

4. The Warrens tried to dispel the spirits using the power of religion.

_____ a. unite

_____ b. scatter

_____ c. contact

5. That only seemed to anger the spirits, for the violence soon <u>escalated</u>.

_____ a. weakened

_____ b. intensified

_____ c. was punished

_____ Score 3 points for each correct C answer.

_____ Score 2 points for each correct O answer.

_____ **Total Score:** Using Words Precisely

Enter the four total scores in the spaces below, and add them together to find your Reading Comprehension Score. Then record your score on the graph on page 197.

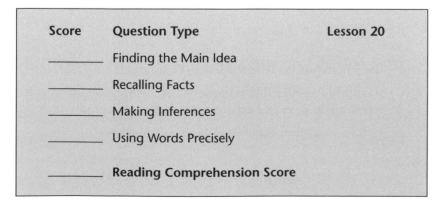

Score	Question Type	Lesson 20
_____	Finding the Main Idea	
_____	Recalling Facts	
_____	Making Inferences	
_____	Using Words Precisely	
_____	**Reading Comprehension Score**	

Author's Approach

Put an X in the box next to the correct answer.

1. What does the author mean by the statement "One [college professor] even brushed Janet off by suggesting she had been watching too many horror movies"?

   ☐ a. The professor thought that Janet was too imaginative.

   ☐ b. The professor was frightened by Janet's story.

   ☐ c. The professor told Janet how to spend her time.

2. The author probably wrote this article in order to

   ☐ a. warn the reader about the forces of the dead.

   ☐ b. explain that spirits often emerge in families with teenagers.

   ☐ c. tell the reader about the Smurls' experience with apparitions.

3. How is the author's purpose for writing the article expressed in paragraph 10?

   ☐ a. The author shows that even prayer had no effect on the spirits.

   ☐ b. The author describes the Smurls' efforts to get rid of the spirits.

   ☐ c. The author suggests that the violence in the Smurl home escalated because of the presence of teenagers.

4. The author tells this story mainly by

   ☐ a. comparing the reaction of college professors and church officials to a reported spirit infestation.

   ☐ b. describing several families' ordeals with spirit infestations.

   ☐ c. retelling one family's personal experiences with spirit infestations.

_____ Number of correct answers

Record your personal assessment of your work on the Critical Thinking Chart on page 198.

CRITICAL THINKING

Summarizing and Paraphrasing

Put an X in the box next to the correct answer.

1. Below are summaries of the article. Choose the summary that says all the most important things about the article but in the fewest words.

☐ a. Destructive and increasingly violent spirits invaded the Smurls' house. The family sought help in many places, but for years no one was able to dispel the spirits.

☐ b. The Smurls wrote a book about their experiences called *The Haunted*, which later became the basis for a popular movie.

☐ c. Four spirits were discovered in the Smurls' house: two women, one man, and a demon. The demon seemed determined to destroy the Smurls.

2. Choose the sentence that correctly restates the following sentence from the article:

"But the Warrens informed them that, in all likelihood, a move would do no good; the spirits would probably follow them wherever they went."

☐ a. The Warrens said that the spirits would probably move soon.

☐ b. The Warrens said that the spirits would probably go with the Smurls if they moved to a new house.

☐ c. The Warrens told the Smurls not to move because it might anger the spirits.

_____ Number of correct answers

Record your personal assessment of your work on the Critical Thinking Chart on page 198.

Critical Thinking

Put an X in the box next to the correct answer for questions 1, 3, and 4. Follow the directions provided for questions 2 and 5.

1. From the information in paragraph 9, you can conclude that

☐ a. teenagers enjoy the attention they receive from spirits.

☐ b. a family with teenagers is more likely to be haunted than one with no children at all.

☐ c. spirits enjoy peace and tranquility.

2. Choose from the letters below to correctly complete the following statement. Write the letters on the lines.

In the article, _____ and _____ are different.

a. the reaction of Ed and Lorraine Warren to the Smurls' story

b. the reaction of college professors to the Smurls' story

c. the reaction of most church leaders to the Smurls' story

3. What was the effect of the Smurls' decision to go public with their story?

☐ a. The spirits finally faded away.

☐ b. They hoped the media attention might attract someone who could help them.

☐ c. Their lives became even more difficult.

4. How is the account of the Smurl haunting an example of a ghost story?

☐ a. The Smurls had teenage children in their home.

☐ b. Strange and terrible things happened at the Smurl house that, it seems, could be explained only by the presence of spirits.

☐ c. A movie was made about the Smurls' experiences.

5. In which paragraph did you find the information or details to answer question 3?

_____

Self-Assessment

I'm proud of how I answered question #_____ in section _____ because

_____

_____

_____

_____

_____ Number of correct answers

Record your personal assessment of your work on the Critical Thinking Chart on page 198.

Personal Response

If I were the author, I would add

_____

_____

_____

_____

because

_____

_____

_____

CRITICAL THINKING

SPIRITUALISM
Fact or Fraud?

This illustration shows the Fox sisters levitating a table at a séance in Rochester, New York, in 1850.

Spiritualism—the belief that a person's spirit survives after death and can communicate with the living through a medium—got its start on Friday, March 31, 1848. On that day two young girls, Margaret and Katherine Fox, reported having the first of a number of "spirit conversations." Those conversations were to make the Fox family, and spiritualism, the talk of the country.

2   In December of 1847, the Fox family moved into a house in the small town of Hydesville, in upstate New York. Within two months, strange rappings began to be heard at all hours—but only when the two girls were present. Margaret and Katherine —or Kate, as she was called—were not at all upset by the noises.

3   Their parents, on the other hand, were distressed, especially their mother, who was a devout Methodist. She was convinced that the sounds were the work of the devil. Hearing that, Margaret and Kate laughingly named the phenomenon "Mr. Splitfoot," because the devil is often pictured as having cloven hooves.

4   Mrs. Fox tried unsuccessfully to find the source of the rappings. Then, on March 31, after the family had gone to

bed, the rappings started up and were so persistent that no one could sleep. One of the children finally sat up and called out, "Here, Mr. Splitfoot, do as I do." She snapped her fingers once and was answered with a single rap. She then snapped her fingers several more times, and was answered with an equal number of raps.

5   By that time the girls' parents had joined them. Together they worked out a simple code. Phrasing questions that could be answered with a yes or no or a number, Mrs. Fox interrogated the knocking intruder. It answered all her questions correctly.

6   The Foxes were informed that Mr. Splitfoot was the spirit of a man who in life had been a peddler. He had supposedly been robbed of five hundred dollars, murdered in that very house, and buried in the cellar.

7   The next day the Foxes tried to check out the story. Town records held no mention of any peddlers being murdered, nor did a search of the cellar yield any bones. What did get out, however, was news of the rappings. Before long the house was crowded with curious folks from all over the Northeast.

8   The excitement in the Fox house became so great that Mrs. Fox sent Margaret and Kate to live with their older sister, Leah, in Rochester. Mrs. Fox hoped that the spirit would not follow the girls, but it did.

9   Since Rochester was a big city, once the news of Mr. Splitfoot got out even greater crowds converged on the Fox sisters. Soon all three sisters were the center of a devoted "spirit circle," which met nightly in Leah's house.

10   Soon the shrewd Leah, who was more than 20 years older than her sisters, conceived the idea of making money from the phenomenon. She arranged a public demonstration in Corinthian Hall, Rochester's largest auditorium. Admission was set at one dollar, a tidy sum in those days.

11   The "rapping telegraph," as the question-and-answer system was dubbed, was a rousing success. Two more meetings were held, both before packed houses. Not everyone was taken with the show, however. Some people set out to prove that the Fox sisters were frauds.

12   Committees were formed to study the performances. Nothing dishonest was discovered. Still, enraged doubters began throwing firecrackers onto the stage and threatening the sisters. The police hustled the women to safety.

13   The sisters began touring, attracting large crowds wherever they performed. They also offered private demonstrations. Their clients included the rich and the famous. Among them was Mary Todd Lincoln, who wished to communicate with her recently assassinated husband, President Abraham Lincoln.

14   As spiritualism spread, arguments for and against it raged. The believers far outnumbered the nonbelievers. Indeed, the harder the skeptics tried to discredit the Fox sisters, the more firmly their supporters believed.

15   Then, on October 21, 1888—40 years after the first incidents at Hydesville—Margaret Fox gave a special demonstration at the Academy of Music in New York City. Her purpose: to confess to defrauding the public. A newspaper account of the day describes the reaction of the audience to the news:

There was a dead silence; everybody in the hall knew they were looking upon the woman who is principally responsible for spiritualism. She stood upon a little pine table, with nothing on her feet but stockings. As she remained motionless, loud distinct rappings were heard, now in the flies, now behind the scenes, now in the gallery.

16   Margaret was making the rapping sounds by snapping a joint in her big toe.

Sir Oliver Lodge devised a test to determine if Dr. Phinuit, a spirit who spoke through Leonora Piper, was genuine.

188

The acoustical properties of the hall gave the illusion that the sounds were coming from different locations.

17   You might think that this astonishing revelation spelled the end of spiritualism, but it didn't. People refused to believe Margaret. They argued that she had been forced into a false confession—by the churches, perhaps, or by the newspapers. And even if the Fox sisters were frauds, they argued, that did not mean that all spiritualists were frauds.

18   Two years later, the sisters retracted the confession and took up their demonstrations once again. Both Margaret and Kate, however, were deep in the grip of alcoholism and died soon after. Only the wily Leah was able to go on, and she did, amassing a small fortune.

19   Given that story, you might reasonably conclude that spiritualism was a hoax. But before you make up your mind, consider the story of Leonora Piper.

20   In 1884 Leonora Piper, plagued by a series of ailments, sought relief from a psychic healer in Boston. Though her first visit offered no relief, Leonora later said that some powerful force commanded her to visit the healer a second time. She did, and that time she felt herself drawn into a trance. Furniture whirled about her, her mind reeled, and she began to speak, but not in her own voice. It was the voice of a dead girl named Chlorine.

21   Soon Leonora learned to enter into a trance at will. Over the next four years she was possessed by a number of spirits, each, it seemed, trying to gain control over her. They included the spirits of some

famous people: actress Sarah Siddons, poet Henry Wadsworth Longfellow, and composer Johann Sebastian Bach.

22   Leonora became the subject of a serious study. William James of Harvard College and Richard Hodgson of the American Society for Psychical Research "adopted" her. From 1887 until 1911, many people interested in spiritualism studied Leonora. Detectives trailed her. People copied down her every word. Every facet of her life was scrutinized for fraud. None was found.

23   During that time one spirit began to dominate Leonora in her trances. It was a spirit who called itself Dr. Phinuit. He spoke English with a heavy French accent.

24   In one of their tests, James and Hodgson assembled a group of people who were introduced to Leonora under false names. When Leonora dropped into a trance, Dr. Phinuit took over. He revealed details about the people that Leonora could not possible have known—including places, dates, and even their real names. Every attempt to throw her off the track failed. The same test was conducted in England by members of the British Society for Psychical Research, with the same results.

25   As one final test, Oliver Lodge, head of the British committee, devised a test he felt would be foolproof. Lodge, it seems, had twin uncles, Robert and Jerry. Jerry had died 20 years earlier. At a séance Lodge showed Dr. Phinuit a gold watch. The doctor spoke at once. "It belonged to your uncle," he said. "Your uncle Jerry." Then followed a rambling conversation

between Lodge and Dr. Phinuit, during which the doctor revealed an astonishing number of anecdotes about the dead Uncle Jerry. Lodge was convinced that Leonora was an extraordinary medium.

26   At the conclusion of the séances, Oliver Lodge and his fellow committee members wrote a detailed report to the British society. They concluded that they had never before met anyone like Leonora Piper. They were in awe of her powers.

27   As for Dr. Phinuit, however, the report stated that he was never a real person. The story of his life was contradictory. His medical knowledge was weak. Phinuit, the report suggested, was a variant of the name used by the Boston psychic whom Leonora first saw. Dr. Phinuit, they concluded, was Leonora's *alter ego*—another side of her personality that she got in touch with only when she entered a trance. She gave him his name unconsciously. There was no attempt at fraud. Her contact with spirits, the British group believed, was genuine.

If you have been timed while reading this article, enter your reading time below. Then turn to the Words-per-Minute Table on page 195 and look up your reading speed (words per minute). Enter your reading speed on the graph on page 196.

Reading Time: Lesson 21

_____ : _____
Minutes   Seconds

Finding the Main Idea

One statement below expresses the main idea of the article. One statement is too general, or too broad. The other statement explains only part of the article; it is too narrow. Label the statements using the following key:

M—Main Idea   **B—Too Broad**   **N—Too Narrow**

_____ 1. The Fox sisters toured the country, claiming that they could contact the dead.

_____ 2. The spiritualism movement, which claimed that spirits can contact the living through an especially sensitive human, included both frauds and seemingly true mediums.

_____ 3. The spiritualism movement raised many questions about supernatural issues.

_____ Score 15 points for a correct M answer.

_____ Score 5 points for each correct B or N answer.

_____ **Total Score:** Finding the Main Idea

 Recalling Facts

How well do you remember the facts in the article? Put an X in the box next to the answer that correctly completes each statement about the article.

1. The Fox sisters lived in
   ☐ a. England.
   ☐ b. New York.
   ☐ c. the Midwest.

2. According to Margaret Fox, the rappings were made by
   ☐ a. Dr. Phinuit.
   ☐ b. snapping her fingers.
   ☐ c. cracking her toe.

3. When Margaret Fox admitted to fraud,
   ☐ a. the belief in spiritualism continued anyway.
   ☐ b. she and her sisters were put in jail.
   ☐ c. the spiritualism movement ended.

4. The spiritualism movement was strong during the
   ☐ a. first half of the 19th century.
   ☐ b. last half of the 19th century.
   ☐ c. early 20th century.

5. When in a trance, Leonora Piper could
   ☐ a. speak foreign languages.
   ☐ b. compose music.
   ☐ c. identify strangers.

Score 5 points for each correct answer.

_____ **Total Score:** Recalling Facts

C Making Inferences

When you combine your own experience and information from a text to draw a conclusion that is not directly stated in that text, you are making an inference. Below are five statements that may or may not be inferences based on information in the article. Label the statements using the following key:

C—Correct Inference   F—Faulty Inference

_____ 1. Leonora Piper is the only medium ever found to be honest.

_____ 2. The Fox sisters all felt guilty for the fraud they engaged in.

_____ 3. In the beginning, Margaret secretly told her two sisters about the trick of cracking her toe.

_____ 4. The psychic researchers forced Leonora to subject herself to their tests.

_____ 5. Many people are fascinated with the subject of spirits.

Score 5 points for each correct answer.

_____ **Total Score:** Making Inferences

D Using Words Precisely

Each numbered sentence below contains an underlined word or phrase from the article. Following the sentence are three definitions. One definition is closest to the meaning of the underlined word. One definition is opposite or nearly opposite. Label those two definitions using the following key. Do not label the remaining definition.

C—Closest   O—Opposite or Nearly Opposite

1. …Margaret and Kate laughingly named the phenomenon "Mr. Splitfoot," because the devil is often pictured as having <u>cloven</u> hooves.

_____ a. foul-smelling

_____ b. divided into two parts

_____ c. unified

2. Indeed, the harder the skeptics tried to <u>discredit</u> the Fox sisters, the more firmly their supporters believed.

_____ a. cast doubt on

_____ b. prove true

_____ c. learn about

3. You might think that this astonishing <u>revelation</u> spelled the end of spiritualism, but it didn't.

_____ a. fraud

_____ b. discovery

_____ c. secret

4. Only the <u>wily</u> Leah was able to go on, and she did, amassing a small fortune.

_____ a. dim-witted

_____ b. shrewd

_____ c. lovely

5. During that time one spirit began to <u>dominate</u> Leonora in her trances.

_____ a. speak with

_____ b. serve

_____ c. control

_____ Score 3 points for each correct C answer.

_____ Score 2 points for each correct O answer.

_____ **Total Score:** Using Words Precisely

Enter the four total scores in the spaces below, and add them together to find your Reading Comprehension Score. Then record your score on the graph on page 197.

Score	Question Type	Lesson 21
_____	Finding the Main Idea	
_____	Recalling Facts	
_____	Making Inferences	
_____	Using Words Precisely	
_____	**Reading Comprehension Score**	

Author's Approach

Put an X in the box next to the correct answer.

1. The author uses the first sentence of the article to

☐ a. tell the reader when spiritualism began.

☐ b. entertain the reader with a story about spiritualism.

☐ c. compare the living world to the spirit world.

2. In this article, "Not everyone was taken with the show, however" means that

☐ a. some people weren't able to go to see the show.

☐ b. not everyone was impressed by the show.

☐ c. many people went to the show alone.

3. Choose the statement below that best describes the author's position in paragraph 18.

☐ a. Of the three Fox sisters, Leah knew best how to take advantage of an opportunity.

☐ b. Margaret and Kate were driven to alcoholism by the spirits they communicated with.

☐ c. The Fox sisters were not fakes.

4. The author probably wrote this article in order to

☐ a. express his or her distaste for spiritualism.

☐ b. persuade the reader to consult a medium.

☐ c. acquaint the reader with both sides of a controversial issue.

_____ Number of correct answers

Record your personal assessment of your work on the Critical Thinking Chart on page 198.

CRITICAL THINKING

Summarizing and Paraphrasing

Follow the directions provided for questions 1 and 2. Put an X in the box next to the correct answer for question 3.

1. Complete the following one-sentence summary of the article using the lettered phrases from the phrase bank below. Write the letters on the lines.

> **Phrase Bank:**
> a. the Fox sisters' "contact" with Mr. Splitfoot
> b. Leonora Piper's experience with spirits
> c. the Fox sisters' performances and eventual confession

    The article about spiritualism begins with _____, goes on to explain _____, and ends with _____.

2. Reread paragraph 25 in the article. Below, write a summary of the paragraph in no more than 25 words.

_____

_____

_____

Reread your summary and decide whether it covers the important ideas in the paragraph. Next, try to shorten the summary to 15 words or less without leaving out any essential information. Write this summary below.

_____

_____

_____

3. Choose the best one-sentence paraphrase for the following sentence from the article:

"Though her first visit offered no relief, Leonora later said that some powerful force commanded her to visit the healer a second time."

☐ a. Even though the first visit had done no good, the healer ordered Leonora to visit him a second time.

☐ b. Even though her first visit had done no good, Leonora felt that a force within her demanded that she return to the healer.

☐ c. Even though her first visit had done no good, Leonora decided on her own that she would visit the healer a second time.

> _____ Number of correct answers
>
> Record your personal assessment of your work on the Critical Thinking Chart on page 198.

Critical Thinking

Follow the directions provided for questions 1 and 3. Put an X in the box next to the correct answer for questions 2 and 4.

1. For each statement below, write O if it expresses an opinion and write F if it expresses a fact.

_____ a. The Fox sisters admitted to being frauds.

_____ b. The British Society for Psychical Research concluded that Leonora Piper was a genuine spiritualist.

_____ c. No one with any intelligence believes in spiritualism.

2. From the article, you can predict that if Leonora Piper had given public demonstrations of her trances,

☐ a. many people would have come to see her.

☐ b. no one would have come to see her.

☐ c. the Fox sisters would have accused her of being a fraud.

3. Using what is told about the Fox sisters and Leonora Piper in the article, name three ways the sisters are similar to and three ways they are different from Leonora. Cite the paragraph number(s) where you found details in the article to support your conclusions.

Similarities

_____

_____

_____

Differences

_____

_____

_____

4. What was a major cause of excitement in the Fox house?

☐ a. The discovery that Mr. Splitfoot was the spirit of a murdered peddler

☐ b. Margaret and Kate's visit to their sister Leah's home

☐ c. The fact that news of the rappings spread throughout the Northeast

_____ Number of correct answers

Record your personal assessment of your work on the Critical Thinking Chart on page 198.

Personal Response

What was most surprising or interesting to you about this article?

_____

_____

_____

_____

Self-Assessment

From reading this article, I have learned

_____

_____

_____

_____

CRITICAL THINKING

Compare and Contrast

Think about the articles you have read in Unit Three. Choose four articles that describe the apparitions you remember best. Write the titles in the first column of the chart below. Use information you learned from the articles to fill in the empty boxes in the chart.

Title	Where and when did this person live?	Whom did he or she haunt?	Would you have liked or disliked this person in life? Explain why.

If there really were ghosts, which people featured in today's news might be tomorrow's apparitions? Why would they come back to haunt the living? What places would they haunt? _____

_____

Words-per-Minute Table

Unit Three

Directions: If you were timed while reading an article, refer to the Reading Time you recorded in the box at the end of the article. Use this words-per-minute table to determine your reading speed for that article. Then plot your reading speed on the graph on page 196.

Lesson / No. of Words	15 / 1428	16 / 1385	17 / 1203	18 / 1522	19 / 1321	20 / 964	21 / 1452	Seconds
1:30	952	923	802	1015	881	643	968	90
1:40	857	831	722	913	793	578	871	100
1:50	779	755	656	830	721	526	792	110
2:00	714	693	602	761	661	482	726	120
2:10	659	639	555	702	610	445	670	130
2:20	612	594	516	652	566	413	622	140
2:30	571	554	481	609	528	386	581	150
2:40	536	519	451	571	495	362	545	160
2:50	504	489	425	537	466	340	512	170
3:00	476	462	401	507	440	321	484	180
3:10	451	437	380	481	417	304	459	190
3:20	428	416	361	457	396	289	436	200
3:30	408	396	344	435	377	275	415	210
3:40	389	378	328	415	360	263	396	220
3:50	373	361	314	397	345	251	379	230
4:00	357	346	301	381	330	241	363	240
4:10	343	332	289	365	317	231	348	250
4:20	330	320	278	351	305	222	335	260
4:30	317	308	267	338	294	214	323	270
4:40	306	297	258	326	283	207	311	280
4:50	295	287	249	315	273	199	300	290
5:00	286	277	241	304	264	193	290	300
5:10	276	268	233	295	256	187	281	310
5:20	268	260	226	285	248	181	272	320
5:30	260	252	219	277	240	175	264	330
5:40	252	244	212	269	233	170	256	340
5:50	245	237	206	261	226	165	249	350
6:00	238	231	201	254	220	161	242	360
6:10	232	225	195	247	214	156	235	370
6:20	225	219	190	240	209	152	229	380
6:30	220	213	185	234	203	148	223	390
6:40	214	208	180	228	198	145	218	400
6:50	209	203	176	223	193	141	212	410
7:00	204	198	172	217	189	138	207	420
7:10	199	193	168	212	184	135	203	430
7:20	195	189	164	208	180	131	198	440
7:30	190	185	160	203	176	129	194	450
7:40	186	181	157	199	172	126	189	460
7:50	182	177	154	194	169	123	185	470
8:00	179	173	150	190	165	121	182	480

Minutes and Seconds

Plotting Your Progress: Reading Speed

Unit Three

Directions: If you were timed while reading an article, write your words-per-minute rate for that in the box under the number of the lesson. Then plot your reading speed on the graph by putting a small X on the line directly above the number of the lesson, across from the number of words per minute you read. As you mark your speed for each lesson, graph your progress by drawing a line to connect the X's.

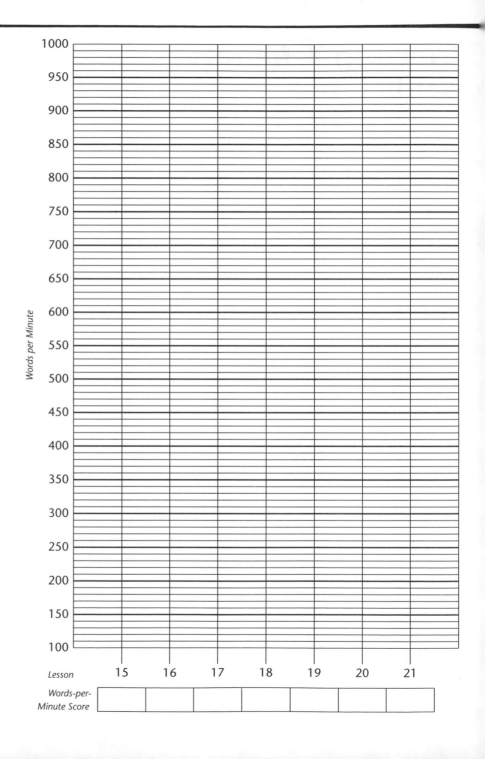

Plotting Your Progress: Reading Comprehension

Unit Three

Directions: Write your Reading Comprehension score for each lesson in the box under the number of the lesson. Then plot your score on the graph by putting a small X on the line directly above the number of the lesson and across from the score you earned. As you mark your score for each lesson, graph your progress by drawing a line to connect the X's.

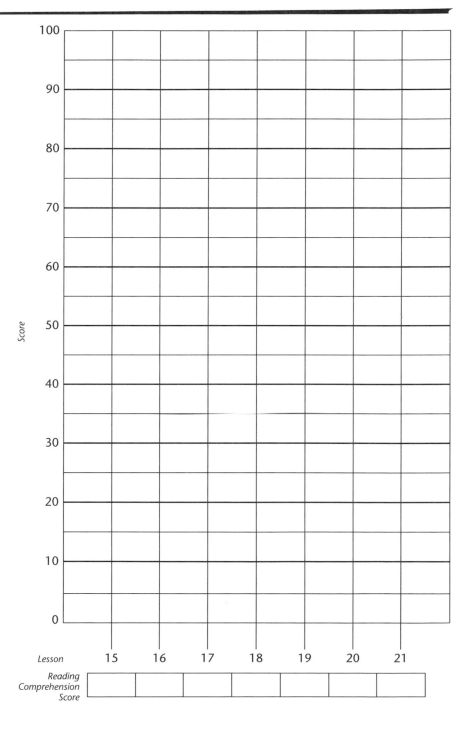

Plotting Your Progress: Critical Thinking

Unit Three

Directions: Work with your teacher to evaluate your responses to the Critical Thinking questions for each lesson. Then fill in the appropriate spaces in the chart below. For each lesson and each type of Critical Thinking question, do the following: Mark a minus sign (–) in the box to indicate areas in which you feel you could improve. Mark a plus sign (+) to indicate areas in which you feel you did well. Mark a minus-slash-plus sign (–/+) to indicate areas in which you had mixed success. Then write any comments you have about your performance, including ideas for improvement.

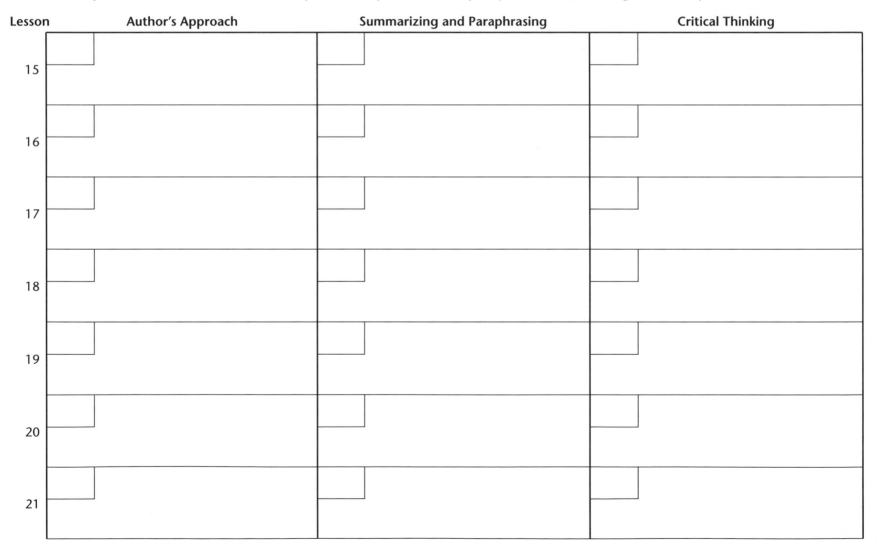

Lesson	Author's Approach	Summarizing and Paraphrasing	Critical Thinking
15			
16			
17			
18			
19			
20			
21			

Picture Credits

Cover: © Arthur Tilley/FPG International

Sample Lesson: pp. 3, 4 UPI/Corbis-Bettmann; p. 5 Archive Photos

Unit 1 Opener: p. 13 Museum of the City of New York/Archive Photos

Lesson 1 pp. 14, 15 Tennessee Tourist Development

Lesson 2 p. 22 UPI/Corbis-Bettmann; p. 23 J. Faircloth/Transparencies, Inc.

Lesson 3 p. 30 George White Location Photography; p. 31 UPI/Corbis-Bettmann

Lesson 4 p. 38 Chris Sorensen; p. 39 AP/Wide World Photos

Lesson 5 p. 46 The Granger Collection; p. 47 Tom Pantages

Lesson 6 p. 54 Museum of the City of New York/Archive Photos; p. 55 Corbis-Bettmann

Lesson 7 p. 54 Fine Art Photographic Library, London/Art Resource, NY; p. 55 Archive Photos

Unit 2 Opener p. 75 Fortean Picture Library

Lesson 8 p. 76 The Granger Collection; p. 77 George White Location Photography

Lesson 9 p. 84 Ben Siegfried; p. 85 AP/Wide World Photos

Lesson 10 p. 92 AP/Wide World Photos; p. 93 Corbis-Bettmann

Lesson 11 pp. 100, 101 Fortean Picture Library

Lesson 12 pp. 108, 109 Winchester Mystery House, San Jose, CA

Lesson 13 p. 116 Giraudon/Art Resource, NY; p. 117 Archive Photos

Lesson 14 pp. 124, 125 Cpr. Jim Markham

Unit 3 Opener p. 137 Stock Montage, Inc.

Lesson 15 pp. 138, 139 Frances G. Beal

Lesson 16 pp. 146, 147 UPI/Corbis-Bettmann

Lesson 17 p. 154 Stock Montage, Inc.; p. 155 Archive Photos

Lesson 18 pp. 162, 163 Michael Dwyer/Stock, Boston

Lesson 19 pp. 170, 171 William Cornett

Lesson 20 p. 178 From: *The Haunted—One Family's Nightmare,* by Robert Curran (with Jack and Janet Smurl and Ed and Lorraine Warren), Copyright 1988, St. Martin's Press, New York; p. 179 AP/Wide World Photos

Lesson 21 pp. 186, 187 Fortean Picture Library